THE SOCIAL CEO

THE SOCIAL CEO

How Social Media Can Make
You A Stronger Leader

DAMIAN CORBET

BLOOMSBURY BUSINESS
LONDON • NEW YORK • OXFORD • NEW DELHI • SYDNEY

BLOOMSBURY BUSINESS
Bloomsbury Publishing Plc
50 Bedford Square, London, WC1B 3DP, UK
1385 Broadway, New York, NY 10018, USA

BLOOMSBURY, BLOOMSBURY BUSINESS and the Diana logo are
trademarks of Bloomsbury Publishing Plc

First published in Great Britain 2019

Cover design by Jason Anscomb / Rawshock Design

A catalogue record for this book is available from the British Library.

A catalog record for this book is available from the Library of Congress.

ISBN: HB: 978-1-4729-6724-4
ePDF: 978-1-4729-6727-5
eBook: 978-1-4729-6725-1

Typeset by Deanta Global Publishing Services, Chennai, India
Printed and bound in Great Britain

To find out more about our authors and books visit www.bloomsbury.com
and sign up for our newsletters.

For Janina

CONTENTS

FOREWORD

Brian Solis

If you're reading this I'm going to make a series of assumptions in your favour. You either get it or you're seeking to get it. Whichever way, you're on the right path.

Being a social CEO takes more than mastering social networks and building a community on social media. It means you believe so much in what *we* as a community stand for, and where we need to go together, that your dreams, aspirations and voice become ours.

Let's forget everything we know about social media for a moment. The world really doesn't need another conversation about social networks. There's always going to be another Facebook, Twitter, LinkedIn – and who knows what's next – which comes and goes with every trend. That's not the point. We all can now appreciate that social media is forever part of our lives. We all have access to amazing platforms where billions of people are connected to one another.

But that doesn't mean everyone has a voice worth following. Nor does it mean everyone deserves an audience.

The signal-to-noise ratio has become deafening. I once said that the good thing about social media is that it gave everyone a voice. The unfortunate thing about it is that *it gave everyone a voice*.

Honestly, the last thing we need is another person on social media just to be on social media – another voice adding to 'the conversation'. And, certainly, no one needs another 'thought leader' or 'expert' posting 'insights' in the hope of boosting their personal brand, collecting followers and likes as if they were a hard currency or fuelling shallow conversations or digital small talk to give the semblance of engagement and community.

We just don't.

Whatever your marketing, social media, PR or communications teams tell you, you don't *have* to have a social media presence. You don't *have* to tweet, post, insta, snap, blog, slack and so on to be present and relevant. You really don't.

But, that's not what Damian is talking about when he refers to the idea of being a social CEO.

It's not just about having a presence on social media or sending branded or corporate approved messages. It's not just about expressing yourself because you have the platforms to do so.

What many get wrong with social media is that the mere *act* of being social contributes to stature. Attention is a precious commodity. We can earn it. We can definitely spend it. But those who listen and learn and set out to create value can earn more than attention. They can build a meaningful and influential community, where the community represents something greater than any one person.

That's what Damian is talking about here: leadership in public view.

Technology by itself doesn't make leaders. Technology only amplifies true leadership.

That must exist within you and it must grow with you as part of a community. Everybody should grow. And, to be honest, that's what the world needs now more than ever. Genuine, human, value-added leadership.

Whomever your community is made up of, whether it's your colleagues, employees, customers, supporters or peers, everyone can benefit from meaning, guidance and leadership.

We all need more signal and less noise. We all need beacons. We all need salient and empathetic voices to move us in a common, rewarding direction.

Being a social CEO is simply an extension of tried and true leadership in the modern social age. Social CEOs use social technologies to lead us in a direction unified by the digital ties that bind us.

That's the thing about social leadership; true leaders don't create followers or seek attention – they empower other leaders.

This is your community. This is our community. And community is much more than leading or belonging to something – it's about doing something together that makes belonging matter.

Let's do this.

PREFACE

This book has contributions from many different people. Some are CEOs; some are former CEOs; some run their own small business; some are consultants; some have written books of their own; some are regular bloggers or contributors to websites like the Huffington Post and Forbes; some have never written an article in their lives.

Their writing styles vary; their backgrounds vary; their outlooks vary; their opinions vary. There is no homogenous 'voice'. They may even disagree with each other sometimes. What they all have in common is a passionate belief in the power of social media for leaders.

This diversity of backgrounds, experience and opinions – and the fact that they may not all agree with each other – is, I believe, the great strength of this book.

This is not accidental. It was a deliberate decision to aim for a wide mix of contributors and to mix things up. I don't want you to go away from this book with a single view of what's 'right'. Instead, I want you to be exposed to multiple views, opinions and experiences. The readers of this book aren't the same; they don't have uniform backgrounds or experiences or needs – so why should the contributors?

Read and enjoy!

Damian Corbet

ACKNOWLEDGEMENTS

There are many people who helped make this book happen.

I have to start by thanking Stephen Waddington, who edited *Share This* and *Share This Too*. The multi-author format of those books got me thinking about doing something similar. Stephen was also kind enough to meet me back in early 2017 to listen to my ideas and encouraged me to go for it.

I'm also very grateful to Isabel de Clercq for inviting me to write a chapter for her book *Social Technologies in Business. Connect – Share – Lead*, which was published in 2018. Isabel proved that the multi-author format was not only possible but worked very well. This spurred me on to get *The Social CEO* completed.

Of course, the book would not have happened without all the amazing contributors, and I have to thank them all for believing in me and for writing their brilliant chapters. In strictly alphabetical order, they are Zoe Amar, Matt Ballantine, David Barker, Chris Bartley, Nicola Brentnall, Michelle Carvill, Mary Curnock Cook, Andrea Edwards, Katie Elizabeth, Paul Frampton Calero, Sarah Goodall, Tammy Gordon, Brett Gosper, Julia Hanigsberg, Samantha Kelly, Oliver Lawal, Tom Marchant, Chris Mason, Jan Owen, Charles Pender, Bob Pickard, Theo Priestley, Euan Semple, David Taylor, Mark Tercek, Martin Thomas, Jack Salzwedel and Brian Solis. It may seem a bit obvious to say that without them the book wouldn't exist, but without them the book wouldn't exist.

I must also thank Emily Bedford, Bloomsbury's commissioning editor at the time I submitted my proposal (she's now moved into fiction publishing), for seeing the book's potential and giving me a chance. Thanks also to her replacement Matt James for guiding me through the latter stages of the editorial process. Also at Bloomsbury, thanks must go to Kealey Ridgen and Emily Crowley Wroe for their sterling help with publicity and Giles Herman, the production editor. Finally, I'd like to thank Leeladevi Ulaganathan, the senior project manager at Deanta Global, for her patience with all my last-minute corrections and changes. I really did take it down to the wire!

I couldn't finish without also mentioning the many people who have helped me along the way – intentionally or otherwise. Some played a part long before the book was even an idea, when I was just toying with the concept of social media for leaders. Whether it was through listening to my ideas and not laughing, giving me encouragement and support, providing speaking opportunities, or kicking my butt, they all helped whether they know it or not. I can't name them all – the list is too long – but I'd particularly like to thank Graeme Leith, Julian Stodd, Henrik Essen, Lina Duque, Kerstin Schinck, Betty Spencer, Andrew Ridge, Simon Bennet, Craig Murray, Mark Fulker, David Waller, Lisa Wallner, Peter Bangham, Katherine Livesey and Rob Dietrich. You all had a hand in it!

CONTRIBUTORS

Brian Solis is a principal analyst at Altimeter Group, a Prophet company. He is also an award-winning author, prominent blogger/ writer and keynote speaker. A digital analyst, anthropologist and futurist, his research and books help executives better understand the relationship between the evolution of technology and its impact on business and society and also the role we each play in it.

Twitter: @briansolis

LinkedIn: @briansolis

Instagram: @briansolis

Website: https://www.briansolis.com/

Damian Corbet is a freelance social media consultant, writer and photographer. He runs The Social C-Suite, which he started in 2014, in order to promote social media to senior leaders. He has interviewed many CEOs for his blog and also speaks at conferences.

Twitter: @DamianCorbet/@TheSocialCSuite

LinkedIn: @damiancorbet

Instagram: @DamianCorbet/@TheSocialCSuite

Website: https://thesocialcsuite.net/

Sarah Goodall is the CEO of Tribal Impact and has over twenty years of experience in B2B marketing, most recently leading social business for SAP in the EMEA region. She founded Tribal Impact in 2015 with the sole mission to support sales and marketing professionals within

B2B organizations who are frustrated with outbound tactics yielding little or no return.

Twitter: @SarahGoodall/@TribalImpact

LinkedIn: @sarahgoodall

Instagram: @sarahgoodall10

Website: https://www.tribalimpact.com/

Andrea Edwards, a award-winning B2B communications professional, works with the world's largest companies on the transformation needed to maximize business growth for the digital age. A passionate communications evangelist and expert in social leadership, content marketing and employee advocacy, she helps businesses understand how they can empower employees to delight customers, grow personal career opportunities and build brand success.

Twitter: @AndreaTEdwards

LinkedIn: @andreatedwards

Instagram: @andreawtbedwards

Website: https://andreatedwards.com/

Blog: http://withoutthebollocks.blogspot.com/

Tammy Gordon is the founder of Verified Strategy, a boutique agency specializing in digital and social media audits, training and strategy. She has trained hundreds of professionals and C-Suite executives in how to more effectively use social media to achieve their goals. Tammy has also presented at SXSW Interactive, MediaPost Social Media Insider Summit, Digiday Brand Summit and the NonProfit Tech Conference.

Twitter: @tammy/@CSuiteSocial

LinkedIn: @tammymgordon

Instagram: @tammygordon/@VerifiedStrategy

Website: http://www.verifiedstrategy.com/

Bob Pickard is Principal of Signal Leadership Communication Inc, a Toronto-based public relations (PR) consultancy serving executives dealing with digital disruption. He provides communications counsel to C-Suite leaders on image, issues, relationships and reputation. Bob is a well-known leader in the global PR industry, having run consulting businesses across international markets working in Canada, the United States, Korea, Japan and Singapore.

Twitter: @BobPickard/@signaleadership

LinkedIn: @bobpickard

Website: http://signaleadership.com/

Blog: https://bobpickard.com/

Chris Bartley is Managing Director and Chief Innovation Officer at Havas Life Medicom. Having come to marketing from computer science, he's an expert in utilizing data to support marketing effectiveness. His work with both start-ups and major global corporations has helped build some of today's biggest health brands.

Twitter: @cambartley

LinkedIn: @chris-bartley-42438a4

Instagram: @cambartley

Nicola Brentnall is Chief Executive of The Queen's Commonwealth Trust. She has been with the organization from inception and has been responsible for the development of the proposition, governance, values, brand and fundraising. Nicola has over twenty years of senior leadership experience in the voluntary sector, working across youth, the arts and mental health. She was awarded an MVO in 2015.

Twitter: @NicolaBrentnall

LinkedIn: @nicola-brentnall-mvo-227a7b41

Instagram: @nicolabrentnall

Euan Semple has been a leader and an influencer in the ever changing field of digital technology for two decades. An early adopter of social media, he implemented one of the world's first enterprise social network systems inside the BBC. Since then he has worked with leaders around the world, helping them rise to the challenge of ever faster change. Euan is the author of *Organizations Don't Tweet, People Do: A Manager's Guide to the Social Web.*

Twitter: @euan

LinkedIn: @euansemple

Instagram: @euansemple

Blog: http://euansemple.com/theobvious

David Taylor is a business communications specialist with over twenty-five years of experience in media, gained from a career in journalism, media relations, PR, marketing, social media training and digital consultancy. He works with a range of organizations, helping them to compete in today's digital marketplace using his business communications system DNAsix®. David also works with enterprise support organizations, training their teams to use the same DNAsix® system.

Twitter: @savvysocialDT

LinkedIn: @davidtaylordnasix

Website: http://the-digital.co/

Zoe Amar

Zoe Amar is co-founder of The Social CEOs awards, which recognizes excellence in social media and digital leadership. She runs the social enterprise Zoe Amar Digital, which helps non-profit leaders drive digital change successfully. She also chairs The Charity Digital Code of Practice, is a trustee of Tech Trust and writes regularly for Digital Leaders and other media.

Twitter: @zoeamar

LinkedIn: @zoeamar

Instagram: @zoeamar

Website: http://zoeamar.com/

Martin Thomas has led high-profile advertising, media, PR and sponsorship agencies. Much of his work is focused on helping organizations respond to the opportunities and challenges posed by digital media. He has written three books on this topic, including *The Financial Times Guide to Social Media Strategy*. He is the course leader on social media for the Institute of Directors.

Twitter: @MartinTmkg

LinkedIn: @martinthomas-marketing

Brett Gosper is the CEO of World Rugby. This followed a career as the CEO of a number of major international advertising/marketing services companies. At World Rugby he has strategic and operational responsibility for rugby's global governing body. Since 2012 Brett has overseen the record-breaking Rugby World Cup 2015 in England; the preparation of Asia's first Rugby World Cup, Japan 2019; Rugby World Cup 2023 in France; the growth of the ten-country HSBC World Rugby Sevens Series and rugby's successful return to the Olympic Games in Rio 2016.

Twitter: @brettgosper

LinkedIn: @brett-gosper-45a63331

Instagram: @brett_gosper

Julia Hanigsberg is the President and CEO of Holland Bloorview Kids Rehabilitation Hospital, Canada's largest paediatric, non-acute academic health sciences centre. A lawyer by training, Julia worked in government and academia before becoming a hospital CEO. She has a passion for children's health and enabling meaningful and healthy futures through care, research and advocacy.

Twitter: @Hanigsberg

LinkedIn: @juliahanigsberg

Instagram: @hanigsberg

Blog: https://hollandbloorview.wordpress.com/

Chris Mason is the CEO of FISITA, the International Federation of Automotive Engineering Societies. Since his appointment in 2014 Chris has overseen the extensive modernization of FISITA, transforming the organization into a leading platform for knowledge exchange within the international automotive and mobility systems engineering community. He is a fellow of the Institute of the Motor Industry and is recognized as an expert leader within his field, regularly contributing to discussions and thought leadership pieces on the evolution of the automotive and mobility industry.

Twitter: @CMasonFISITA

LinkedIn: @chrismason11

David Barker, with over twenty-five years of management and senior leadership experience, now juggles life as a charity CEO, consultant, writer, trustee and volunteer supporting charities and not-for-profit organizations across the UK. As an active social CEO, he believes that the best way to learn to become one is to simply dive in and just get on with it.

Twitter: @davidbarkerceo/@YouthTalkCEO

LinkedIn: @david-barker-20a4731

Website: http://www.thrivecharityconsulting.com/

Jack Salzwedel is Chair and CEO of the American Family Insurance enterprise, which includes the American Family brand and its subsidiaries. Jack and his wife, Sarah, created the Slife Institute for Social Work Consultation, Research and Training at Wartburg College. They also established the Salzwedel Family Foundation. Jack serves on several boards in his industry and community. CEO.com has called him the most engaged Fortune 500 CEO on Twitter.

Twitter: @AmFamJack

LinkedIn: @jacksalzwedel

Jan Owen is a social entrepreneur, innovator, influencer and author. As the CEO of the Foundation for Young Australians, she has led the organization's strategic mission to equip young people to create, lead and thrive into the future. She was recognized as one of Australia's 'True Leaders' in 2018 and the Inaugural Australian Financial Review and Westpac 'Woman of Influence' in 2012. She is the author of *Every Childhood Lasts a Lifetime* and *The Future Chasers*.

Twitter: @JanOwenAM

LinkedIn: @jan-owen-b854a828

Mark Tercek was the CEO of The Nature Conservancy, the world's largest conservation organization, between 2008 and 2019. Prior to that he was a partner and managing director of Goldman Sachs, where he worked for twenty-four years. He is the author of the best-selling book *Nature's Fortune: How Business and Society Thrive by Investing in Nature.*

Twitter: @MarkTercek

LinkedIn: @marktercek

Blog: https://www.nature.org/en-us/what-we-do/our-insights/insights-from-mark-tercek/

Katie Elizabeth is the founder and CEO of Stella Digital, a Silicon Valley company that designs and develops customer-facing technology products. She is also the founder of a stealth mode start-up that aims to create global catalysts for positive change.

Twitter: @keKatie

LinkedIn: @kekatie

Mary Curnock Cook is an education expert with a portfolio of non-executive roles. From 2010 to 2017 she was Chief Executive of UCAS. She is on the Boards of the Open University, the Student Loans Company, United Learning, Founders4Schools, the Access Project and LKMCo. Mary is also an investor/mentor to a number of EdTech entrepreneurs. She was awarded an OBE in 2000 and has honorary degrees from Birkbeck, Goldsmiths and the University of Gloucestershire.

Twitter: @MaryCurnockCook

LinkedIn: @mary-curnock-cook-0107bb1

Oliver Lawal is the CEO of AquiSense Technologies, a clean-tech start-up leading new market growth in water treatment products for B2B clients. He previously served in executive positions for two large corporations (Xylem and Halma) living in UK, Germany, France and New Zealand before moving to the United States in 2005.

Twitter: @O_2the_L

LinkedIn: @oliver-lawal-6877ab9

Paul Frampton Calero is the EMEA CEO for travel tech start-up Hi Incorporated and also leads B2C strategy globally. Previously, Paul was the CEO of Havas Media Group where he oversaw a £100m business with 900 staff and 10 operating companies. He is a passionate ambassador for diversity and inclusion and plays an active voice for youth as Chair of Big Youth Group, an organization designed to improve the odds for young people globally.

Twitter: @Paul_Framp

LinkedIn: @paulframpton

Instagram: @framptonunplugged

Charles Pender served two terms as Mayor of Corner Brook, Newfoundland and Labrador. Under his leadership the city undertook a number of major infrastructure projects with an environmental focus. He is a retired educator and post-secondary administrator. He first joined Twitter in 2009 and remains active on social media.

Twitter: @charlespendercb

LinkedIn: @charles-p-097ba53b

Tom Marchant is an entrepreneur known for creating cutting-edge luxury travel and lifestyle brands. He is owner and co-founder of The

Black Tomato Group, including travel companies Black Tomato and Epic Tomato and global creative agency Studio Black Tomato. Black Tomato has been identified by *The New York Times*, *Vogue* and *Condé Nast Traveller* as a leader in luxury travel.

Twitter: @TommyMarchant

LinkedIn: @tom-marchant-4821523

Instagram: tommymarchant10

Samantha Kelly is a social media strategist, international speaker, author and trainer. She is also the founder of the Women's Inspire Network, connecting and empowering female-led businesses and hosting a biannual national conference for female entrepreneurs.

Twitter: @Tweetinggoddess

LinkedIn: @tweetinggoddess

Facebook: @tweetinggoddess

Website: https://www.tweetinggoddess.com/

Matt Ballantine is an independent advisor and consultant to technology, marketing and HR leaders across a broad range of sectors in the United Kingdom, Europe and the United States. He focuses on how technology is changing the way we work and how we need to adapt structures and ways of working to take best advantage. He also presents and produces a number of successful podcasts and is a contributor to Forbes.

Twitter: @ballantine70

LinkedIn: @mattballantine

Blog: https://mmitii.mattballantine.com/

Theo Priestley is recognized as a thought leader and keynote speaker on emerging technologies. He is also a well-known technology evangelist and 'antifuturist', focusing on emerging trends and their impact on business and wider society. He asks the harder questions to deconstruct the paths we are currently taking to build a future for everyone.

Twitter: @tprstly

LinkedIn: @theopriestley

Website: https://www.theopriestley.com/

Michelle Carvill is a strategic marketer, digital agency founder and three-times published author in the digital marketing and social media space. Her latest book *#GetSocial – Social Media Strategy and Tactics for Leaders* helps leaders take a strategic perspective to social technologies – harnessing connected communications both internally and externally.

Twitter: @michellecarvill

LinkedIn: @michellecarvill

Instagram: @michellecarvill

Website: https://www.michellecarvill.com/

Introduction

Damian Corbet

The route to this book has been circuitous and taken almost five years. The original idea of promoting social media to senior leaders came to my mind in 2014, when I was invited to give a presentation on social media to C-level leaders as part of my previous employer's executive training programme.

I thought the attendees would be sceptical at best – and downright hostile at worst – to the idea of using social media, especially Twitter (which was my main focus). Quite the opposite happened. While most of them were complete strangers to Twitter, they were intrigued by the idea of tweeting. Apparently they were all talking about Twitter at breakfast the next day!

This positive response got me thinking: if these senior leaders from a very traditional manufacturing organization thought Twitter wasn't a completely crazy idea, perhaps leaders from other businesses would be open to social media too.

It's been quite a journey since then. I started by creating social media accounts (under the name 'The Social C-Suite') and by building Twitter lists of CEOs and other C-level leaders who were active on the platform. I began a 'Social CEO of the Week' column on my blog. People liked it and I was getting lots of retweets and positive comments. I then decided to take it one step further and started interviewing social CEOs – asking them why they used social media and what they got out of it. I dabbled with the idea of a social CEO summit and a social network for CEOs. This was all done in my spare time, as I held down a full-time job to pay the bills.

The summit and social network didn't happen (maybe they will one day!), but the interviews continued, and I've now interviewed almost thirty CEOs for my blog. That may not sound like a lot, but it's been enough to give me a very good insight into the very real benefits they get from social media. There have been many recurring themes in all the interviews – enough, I believe, to confidently say that social media engagement is now essential for the modern leader.

The one feature that all my interviewees have in common is *transparency*. For them, being on social media allows them to display a new kind of leadership – open leadership. They aren't hidden in a corner office; they aren't protected by an executive assistant – they are out there in the digital space. This is revolutionary stuff.

Transparent, open leadership is a relatively new concept – and one that has really started to take off with the advent of social media. It's a revolution, no doubt about that.

Where this revolution is leading is difficult to say, but now that the genie is out of the bottle there's no going back. A new generation of leaders are embracing the openness that social media allows – and they are running with it. These social leaders are still in the minority, but their numbers are growing rapidly – as is their influence. They are the standard-bearers for Leadership 2.0 (or is it 3.0?).

Those leaders who have embraced social media have, metaphorically, moved from the corner office into the lobby. By relocating, they can see their customers, partners, supporters, employees and competitors come and go and hear their conversations, gripes, needs and aspirations. You don't get that kind of exposure if you're locked away from the real world with an executive assistant guarding your door (and your email). Today's most effective leaders throw open the door and listen to digital buzz around them.

Don't get me wrong, in the Social Age you need to have filters in place – otherwise the noise can be deafening – but you still need to listen and engage. Social media has changed everything – and those leaders who start tapping into it now will reap the benefits.

In this book, by inviting carefully selected contributors – with many of them being CEOs – to discuss this new social leadership revolution, I hope to enlighten, entertain and ultimately inspire you on your own leadership journey. Embrace this powerful new tool and become one of the growing band of leaders who are taking the world of work by storm. If you don't, I feel you may become irrelevant. It's that important.

How the book is structured

The book has four main sections. You can read them in any order you like – or just choose the chapters which seem most relevant to you.

Part One consists of only a single chapter, in which Sarah Goodall describes the Social Age we're now living in and the implications of social media for leaders. I do recommend that everyone reads this chapter, as it puts everything into context and lays the groundwork for the rest of the book.

Part Two looks at the different ways that CEOs and other leaders can utilize social media. Starting with Andrea Edwards's opener on the importance of listening and engaging, there follow chapters – each written by leading experts in the field – on personal branding, PR, social selling, attracting talent, engaging with supporters (for nonprofits), running a small- or medium-sized business, internal engagement with employees and managing risk.

In Part Three, social CEOs from a range of sectors share their insights, expertise and advice. I've tried to include leaders from as wide a range of industries as possible, so hopefully there's something for everyone: sports, healthcare, manufacturing, charities, insurance, social enterprises, the environment, start-ups, education, business-to-business, tech, municipal, travel and small businesses.

Part Four looks to the future. It starts with Matt Ballantine's chapter, where he asserts that social media is, in a way, the ultimate form of disruption for leaders. Building from this, Theo Priestley then looks at how technology is evolving and how this is affecting people in leadership positions. Finally, Michelle Carvill discusses the future of leadership and how you need to continuously adapt and evolve to stay relevant in the Social Age.

I think there's something for everyone in this book. Whether you are a seasoned CEO with decades of experience behind you or are a newly appointed chief executive just getting to grips with your first senior role; whether you work in the commercial or the nonprofit sector; whether you are studying full time for an MBA at business school or attending night classes in management; whether you run your own small business from home or lead a start-up; whether you know about social media or not. Everyone should find something useful to take away and implement on their own social media journey.

I'll finish the Introduction with a quote from Jan Owen,[1] CEO of the Foundation for Young Australians (and one of the contributors to this book) from an interview I did with her back in 2016:

> Social media is one of my KPIs. I use it to keep track of conversations in the sector and the work of colleagues in other organizations; to access breaking news; to share what I'm doing; and to generally stay connected and 'in touch with the zeitgeist'.

So don't put it off – get in touch with the zeitgeist of your industry by embracing social media now!

PART ONE

THE SOCIAL AGE

1

What is the Social Age?

Sarah Goodall

When did you last check your phone? Five minutes ago? Maybe an hour ago? Yesterday? It's unlikely it was yesterday.

The average smart device user will check their phone twenty-eight times a day. That's at least once an hour and more than 10,000 times a year.

We live in a connected age. Advances in technology, changes in working practices and increasing expectations are forcing modernization – both within the workplace and in our daily lives.

These changes are having a profound impact on organizations, challenging them to change how they operate on many levels. Leaders are pivotal in these changes, and these changes in turn require a new style of leadership – one that is open and transparent and is based on trust.

Social media is at the heart of the technological changes that are driving this modern, more collaborative style of leadership. It is the 'how' that allows the modern leader to be found and to engage with their following, wherever they are.

It is the listening platform that flattens hierarchies and connects stakeholders directly to positions of power, simply because the medium is available for all to see.

This shift in technology and, subsequently, the way we communicate has dramatically altered the expectations people have of organizational leaders.

Audiences expect transparency, honesty and ethical standards at all levels of an organization. When high expectations are missed or misjudged, social media is the go-to public platform for airing disagreement.

It is this unpredictable nature of social media that, understandably, deters leaders from engaging online. Risks of 'unwanted attention' and 'negative feedback' are some of the key reasons why leaders are so reluctant to adopt a social approach.

However, these digital conversations are happening, whether the organization is involved or even aware of them. While social media presents unpredictable risk to an organization, it also presents immense opportunity.

The Social Age is disruptive, uncomfortable and happening now. Let's explore the fundamental changes that have caused this to happen and how it impacts your role as a leader.

From IT as a department to a fundamental foundation

The past twenty years have seen a rapid development in telecommunications and the internet and the many applications relying on this technology, including email and social media, which are now ubiquitous.

These technological changes, and the applications they enable, have changed the rules for businesses and organizations worldwide. Services are now available anywhere there is a phone signal or a Wi-Fi connection. They're on your laptop, your phone, your watch. They are even available through the voice-activated smart speaker sitting in the corner of your room. They're enabling connectivity at a scale we could never have imagined before.

And this technology never sleeps, so we can communicate at any time we choose, leaving messages, pictures and videos for connections to pick up at a time they choose.

Communications can be direct, instant, at scale, unfiltered, borderless and virtually cost-free, meaning we can communicate as much and as often as we want, with whoever we want, no matter where they are in the world.

Social media has enabled the establishment of virtual communities which grow through common purpose and beliefs. For organizations, this can mean a loss of control over the communities they previously 'owned', as these communities move away from managed forums and onto social media platforms and more open community sites.

Social technologies cannot be viewed as infrastructure as they are not owned by the organization, but embracing them opens a huge potential for growth. It does, however, mean working with technology you don't control, accepting third-party house rules and realizing that negative commentary can be published for all to see.

But losing control isn't necessarily a bad thing. As an influential leader, your social presence will massively impact your ability to reach a wider community with your message and deepen relationships at scale with a more personal approach to communication.

You begin to extend your, and your organization's, brand beyond existing communities, creating fans and advocates who align with your message and want to follow your story. These fans and advocates are where you will find your future volunteers, employees, customers or members.

Understanding how to manage the risk and what to expect from moving towards openness will be covered by Martin Thomas later in this book.

From formal frameworks to collective communities

Traditional organizations have always led with formal structures based on a hierarchical arrangement of roles and relationships between units and departments.

For many years, these structures have been designed to enable the efficient cascade of information down and the reporting of information back up. They are also perfectly aligned to managing career progression paths, with positions of leadership often reflecting seniority and management responsibility.

However, such structures are highly susceptible to manipulation, with filtering of information in both directions. Individuals may choose not to pass information down the chain because they deem it unnecessary or of personal strategic use. In the same way, information may not pass up the chain in order to hide mistakes from senior management or to prevent others from taking responsibility for a great job.

Modern leaders who embrace the Social Age are suddenly equipped with the means to send out the message they want, to whoever they want and whenever they want. They are also able to get feedback from anyone, in its rawest format. Scary, but essential for any modern leader.

Suddenly, leaders are part of a wider unfiltered conversation that drives innovation, action and often resolution. Communities value this direct relationship with someone in a position of authority. They begin to feel more engaged and connected with the brand at a more human level.

Moreover, embracing a social culture across the organization will enable new leaders to rise. Not leaders in the traditional sense, promoted into a role, but leaders who attract a following through what they say and do and leaders who gain the respect of the community for their experience and the value they give back to the community. Leaders with passion and purpose become influential both inside and outside of the organization.

The Social Age is disrupting organizational structures beyond all recognition as communities form across borders, time zones and interests. They're unstructured, organic and driven by common interests. It's where changemakers rise, and audiences follow. Embracing this approach will liberate creativity and innovation across your organization in ways you have never experienced before.

The ability to stay closely connected to the people that matter most to their organization is what drives most social CEOs to use social media. Andrea Edwards will further explore why listening to and engaging on social media is important to the future role of leadership.

From 'knowledge is power' to lifelong learning

According to the World Economic Forum, 65 per cent of children entering primary school today will ultimately end up working in a role that does not currently exist. With that in mind, how do we educate the communities of tomorrow?

Historically we would rely on libraries, scholars and professors to keep our knowledge informed and current. This higher level of education elevated individuals into positions of power both within government and organizations.

The Social Age has changed our relationship with learning. It's enabling communities to learn with and from each other, when and how they wish to. This shift in trustworthy sources is driven by the ease with which people can use technology to connect and communicate. In an era of 'fake news', we lean towards our trusted networks to provide clarity.

Global influencers are emerging at an unprecedented rate, based not on their academic knowledge but on their experience and ability to communicate. YouTube and Instagram have bred celebrities that are considered more trustworthy to some demographics than friends.

The Social Age is noisy, intrusive and full of irrelevant messages. The challenge (and indeed the skill) now lies in the ability to decipher what is relevant and then act upon it with haste.

Ultimately, it's the responsibility of the social CEO to build high-performing teams and unlock digital potential within their organization. Understanding how to discover answers, collaborate in communities, distil what is relevant and interpret that information with speed is what employees will need to learn to be successful in digital cultures.

Digitally upskilling the organization and providing the technology that will enable a learning culture will be critical to success. But it's this transition that will ultimately liberate creativity and innovation across the organization.

Understanding internal engagement and human-centred cultures will be explored later in this book by Euan Semple.

From listing to living brand values

The Social Age provides a level of transparency that we have never seen before. Organizations operate under the shadow of their latest ratings on Trustpilot and Glassdoor. Branding can no longer be managed via press relations and orchestrated media engagements, but with agile responses and authentic voices.

We now have glass walls surrounding our organizations. Conversations on social media are public, immediate and visible. We must move beyond listing our values as essential must-haves, towards living them wholeheartedly throughout everything we do. Anything other than ethically sound and moral cultures is likely to be exposed through the raw and unfiltered channel of social media.

Such instances are all too familiar. The #MeToo movement quickly spread across social media, gathering momentum from the celebrities of Hollywood to the everyday workplace. Twitter no longer considers itself as a social media channel but a news channel. The viral nature of topical content can be challenging for leaders if they are not prepared.

The social CEO understands the challenge this presents – as well as the opportunity. The Social Age requires leaders to be ready and answerable to their communities. The accessibility and openness of social leadership builds trust and credibility with both internal and external stakeholders. This starts at the top.

Employees look to leadership as an example of what is achievable, what is expected and what is the future. Throughout Part Two of this book you will learn how social CEOs have embraced the Social Age and are transitioning the way they communicate to their stakeholders in more accessible ways.

From command and control to trusted authenticity

Trusted authenticity is critical to social leadership. In an age of fake news, we question the credibility of what brands, governments and, indeed, the social media platforms themselves tell us. We know that newsfeeds are filtered so we turn to our trusted networks, peers and people like ourselves with the decisions we're making.

The Social Age has massively shifted our perception of trusted authority. Controlled messages cascading down the organizational hierarchies via emails, town halls and kick-off events are considered staged, scripted and planned.

The same is true for public relations. Controlling messages that are released to the market is becoming increasingly difficult for organizations. Information leaks, whistle-blowers and mistakes can cause an unexpected crisis for the unprepared leader. However, with technology moving at the pace it is, this will only become more difficult for organizations to control. Bon Pickard talks more about public relations in his chapter.

Relinquishing control is a nervous first step for any CEO. It is an unknown, but necessary step.

Once you choose to empower your internal community to become social advocates, you will create authenticity at scale. However, asking our communities to advocate on behalf of our brands will be difficult if they don't understand how to tell the brand story or, more importantly, where they fit within that story.

Authenticity is key to garnering trust and influence on social media. Understanding individual purpose, telling stories and listening to others will differentiate the social CEO from others. It is all right to be authentically imperfect on social media from time to time. It makes us human – and that's credible. More importantly, it grants your employees permission to learn in the same way.

Later in the book you will learn how controlling your personal brand on social media is more beneficial than leaving it to chance.

Conclusion

Social technologies allow organizations to connect remote teams around the world, facilitate flexible working, deepen relationships at scale and create collaborative environments based around skills and passions (not necessarily office locations).

What's more, changes in social attitudes, largely contributed by social networking behaviours, are driving this expectation within the modern-day workforce. According to the Harvard Business Review, by 2025, approximately 75 per cent of the global workforce will be millennials. This will be a digitally native generation that expects digital working practices as standard. Nicola Brentnall will go further into why attracting best-fit talent via social media is key to organizational growth.

Change is happening, and it will continue. It's disruptive, challenging and uncomfortable. It's time to get comfortable with being uncomfortable.

Modern leaders recognize the trends discussed in this chapter and embrace social technologies to reach out and engage with their stakeholders, be they employees, volunteers, customers or fans. Leaders who choose not to embrace social media will run the risk of becoming increasingly irrelevant and out of touch with their audience.

Ultimately, it's a choice. Your choice. Whether you choose to be disrupted or you disrupt through social leadership.

PART TWO

HOW CAN CEOs USE SOCIAL MEDIA?

2

Listening, engaging and leading

Andrea Edwards

The transformative power of social media happens when it is embraced from the very top of an organization – and then right across it. It is only when every CEO genuinely embraces social media that we will see a fundamental shift in how we do business and how we run our organizations. This shift will make businesses and organizations more successful while also improving societal standards across the world.

It is time for all of us to lead socially and to be more authentic, more passionate and more giving. It is time to open ourselves up, to be vulnerable, to smash down unhelpful silos and hierarchies – and to knock down the PR walls we've been hiding behind for decades. It is time to join the digital arena, because when we do, we are truly capable of understanding our audiences. When we embrace this opportunity, we understand it is how we can grow our businesses/ organizations in what Sarah Goodall describes as the Social Age in the opening chapter of this book. An age of collaboration, of service and of engagement – out there in the digital world.

Whether you're reading this as a business CEO, a leader of a charity, a government official, educator, healthcare leader or any other leader, being a social CEO is about engaging in meaningful conversations with your audience: customers, prospects, partners, shareholders, stakeholders, influencers, employees and your wider community, in their world, where they are actively participating in and influencing *their* communities.

Social leadership is the cornerstone of real transformation – through the voices of its leaders and its people. But you'll never understand it or appreciate its transformative power until you join in and embrace it yourself, as a social CEO.

Research leads the way

In 2013, McKinsey published a report, entitled 'Six social-media skills every leader needs'.[1] Yes – 2013. And still, to this day, 60 per cent of leaders of Fortune 500 companies have no presence on social media at all. None.

In the report, McKinsey stated that any business that develops a critical mass of leaders who master the skills of social media will experience significant business benefits.

Any business whose leaders embrace social media will

- be more creative, innovative and agile;
- be able to attract and retain the best talent;

- have the ability to tap deeper into the capabilities and ideas of employees and stakeholders;

- be more effective at collaborating across internal and external boundaries;

- enjoy a higher degree of global integration – which is critical for the future of borderless business;

- have tighter and more loyal customer/stakeholder relationships, as well as the greater brand equity that comes with it;

- play a leading role in their industries by better leveraging the capabilities of partners in co-creation, co-development and overall industry collaboration;

- be more likely to create new business models that capitalize on the potential of evolving communication technologies;

- empower the business to confront the shortcomings of traditional organization design;

- develop the enabling infrastructure that fosters truly strategic use of social technologies;

- initiate a positive loop, allowing leaders to capitalize on the opportunities and disruptions that come with the community of a networked society; and

- achieve a competitive advantage.

Considering this paper was published in 2013 and that the benefits (when a critical mass of leaders embrace social media) are remarkable, as we move rapidly towards 2020, isn't it surprising that so many leaders and businesses are still not on board?

The benefits are enormous

Being a social CEO changes the way you think. It changes the way you work. It changes your business or organization from such a core foundational place – because you can't simply be internally focused when you're social. Instead, you'll be connected to the global conversation taking place in your industry. This external focus is the pillar to transform your business into a people-focused culture that benefits your greater business community. It is the core tool of transformation today, because it is about communication – the essence of being human.

Overstating it? No. Hard to achieve? Definitely not. The one thing I hear from leaders all the time is that, while they want to do it, they want to make sure they do it well. They don't want to look foolish. When leaders tell me this I am relieved because, yes, doing it well is critical.

To illustrate this point, read this extensive case study[2] I published with IBM in Asia Pacific to detail how the roll-out of a culture change around social leadership impacts a business – right across the business. It is completely transformational, not just for leaders but for all employees as well.

It starts at the top

When we have CEOs active on social media, we give employees the permission to own their voice too. We open up genuine two-way communication with customers, partners, stakeholders and the wider community we seek to influence and engage with.

We also have leaders who are genuinely connected to the conversation and concerns of the communities they want to reach, influence and serve. This transformation must start at the top – with the leaders of business.

Trust

To explore why becoming a social CEO is so critical, we must discuss the importance of trust in the digital age, because right now we are living through a time of great distrust in our leaders.

For insight into trust in the digital economy, you could do worse than reading Edelman's Trust Barometer.[3] A unique piece of research, it has been published annually for nearly two decades and lays out the challenges of trust across business, government, NGOs and the media. Unsurprisingly, media is the most untrusted sector in the world according to the research, with government coming in close behind. Across the board, the research revealed 'a world of seemingly stagnant distrust'.

The most interesting takeaway from the report in recent years is that, while businesses and organizations have gained and lost trust in the last two decades, there is now an opportunity to lead the global conversation around the most pressing issues humanity is facing. Yes, businesses are now *expected* to lead the world towards the change needed, because we don't trust the media or governments to do it anymore.

This requires a leadership mindset that is about re-earning and retaining lost trust. It is not carrying on with business as usual.

Trust must become a strategic priority for all leaders. To lead like this, genuine opportunity lies in becoming a social CEO, driving the conversation on digital channels in meaningful and authentic ways.

But it's not just in leading the conversation where CEOs can succeed. It is also in listening to your audience and participating in conversations too. Social is fundamentally two-way and we must move away from the one-way mindset so common today.

Edelman's Trust Barometer had a clear call-to-action – which is that the decline in trust has given leaders a second chance to regain it. This is due to falling trust in the other categories measured. Right now, understanding the importance of trust, and keeping it, is an opportunity and a strategic imperative.

The other trusted parties in the research are 'technical experts' and 'academic experts'. It was a relief to see 'the experts' regain trust, following UK MP Michael Gove's infamous statement in the lead up to the Brexit vote that the UK had 'had enough of experts'. History consistently reflects that it is a dangerous world when we don't believe the experts!

However, while seeing a decline in trust – which I believe is due to the 'fake news' crisis and our repeated errors to check the sources we share – people like me were still the third most trusted category. This means that the employees or volunteers working for businesses or organizations are an important resource for brands.

With leaders, trust is achieved by demonstrating integrity and authenticity and delivering real value. This can be amplified by empowering the people of your organization to own their own voices too.

So, while understanding that trust is the central pillar of this opportunity, how a leader builds their social media presence is critical. It is not PR. It is not sales messages. It is not marketing. It is not interrupting your customers or supporters with noise. It requires adding real, relevant value.

Where is the customer today?

When I use the term 'customer', of course, I am speaking about the customer for your information – your relevant audience. And we are all customers today, with thousands of brands and organizations vying for our attention and wallets. We are all inundated with information – and very rarely is the quality good enough for us to pay attention or spend time with it.

Just think of the last time you were watching an inspirational video and, in the middle of it, an advert breaks in – an advert you can't skip – and you either stop watching the video or ignore the ad and simply wait for it to finish. This is very rarely a positive experience with a brand or organization.

All it does is move a customer deeper inside their 'bubbles of trust' – the community we want to hear from and be influenced by. This includes family, friends, bloggers, broader social media connections and colleagues. Outside the bubble of trust, trying to break in, are the media, charities, religious leaders, celebrities, brands and politicians.

Of course, the significant difference between the first group and the second – apart from the first being human – is that the second group want something from us: to buy from them, donate to them, believe in them, idolize them, endorse them, vote for them. In the old information age, this second group completely owned the information channels. We, the people, had no control over what we accessed, and alternative viewpoints were harder to come by.

Today, we are much more in control of our information channels. While this is not necessarily a perfect situation (we still tend to exist within 'silos of thought', or the algorithms are feeding us content that backs up what we already think), it is where the customer is today, barricaded against the noise and division of public discourse.

To reach our relevant audiences, we must therefore earn the right to be inside their bubbles of trust. This is the opportunity for leaders today: to understand this fundamental shift by audiences, who are closing themselves off to noise and dissent. Closing themselves off to product pitches and marketing fluff.

That means we must go to them, where they are – online. But we also need to be relevant and earn the right to be in their bubbles. The public is fickle and is not very good at giving second chances today, so we can lose the right to be participate very quickly if we get it wrong.

Understand this and you will change your business.

Don't outsource

This is one of the main reasons why I don't agree with outsourcing your digital voice (apart from having a support team to offer advice and practical help). As an example, Richard Branson is famously dyslexic, so creating perfect prose is probably not something that comes easily to him – so we must assume he has a support team who dot the i's and cross the t's. But do you doubt he is the voice behind his presence? I believe he is very clearly behind his voice – and all CEOs who want to succeed on social media *must* be behind their voice, even if they don't create the final product that goes live.

We are living in a world inundated with noise – often referred to 'infobesity'. A large part of this noise is content created for content's sake. Additionally, when people are not behind their voice, it's obvious to most of us. Like so much of the infobesity out there, it's bland, it's fluff, it's too vanilla. It literally washes past us, because it has no guts, no presence or no meaning.

This is why we're in the era of content shock – the idea that we *must* participate. But far too many have no substance behind their participation, which is turning people off social media and broader engagement beyond their *bubbles of trust*. No one has time to spend with vanilla content! The world is saturated with it.

We created more content in the first decade of this century than has been created in all of human history. It's now doubling every two years. It really is a case of infobesity! The leaders of businesses, therefore, must be very conscious of what they are creating and putting out into the world.

So, make sure you stand for something. Believe in it. Then put all of your amazing energy behind it, so people want to join your cause and share your message, which is how you break through. Which is how you build businesses. Make your voice count. Make it unmissable.

Social CEOs who are succeeding at this – like those who have contributed to this book – have a huge passion for their community and they relish the opportunity to share their views and participate in conversations online. They are inspired and impassioned. They want to serve their audience and share their message. This speaks to us. We know they are doing it because they care.

Let's raise the bar

When you outsource your voice, it never comes across as completely genuine, because *you* are not there. It's impossible for it to contain your magic, because *only you* can capture that. And worse, it diminishes the value of social media. So, if you really want to build something powerful, outsource everything else, but not this. We are in the age of authenticity, and our audience is smart. They see through everything.

Additionally, when you outsource, you are only focused on pushing information out. When you participate, you'll appreciate that this is where the true magic of social media lies – in the engagement and conversations.

Own your voice. Serve your audience. Make it about them. Make it count. Make it meaningful. That's how you break through. That's when people will believe in you and your message.

The importance of the Giving Economy

And this leads nicely on to what I am probably most passionate about on social media: joining the 'Giving Economy'.

Ask yourself these questions: What have you given on social media this week? No, really, what? Who have you praised? Who have you honoured? Who have you elevated? Whose blog have you shared or commented on? What have you given to someone else this week on social media?

The Giving Economy is about lifting others up, delivering value to your community, making someone's life better. It's about giving and sharing. It's not about selling something, even if that something is you.

If you do it well, you can bask in the glory of a stunning digital presence. People will want to be connected with you because you give them something: knowledge, wisdom, praise, recognition and more.

A social CEO is active on social media regularly – if not every day then at least few times a week. Here are seven things they could be doing:

1 Praising an employee for a job well done

2 Sharing or commenting on a blog a colleague has written

3 Interacting with a customer, perhaps by sharing valuable insights relevant to their industry, demonstrating they know the customer and understand their challenges

4 Promoting an article published by a partner, because it's aligned to their business and it's an opportunity to celebrate an awesome partner

5 Sharing a 'thought leadership' piece an influencer has published that they agree with, commenting on why they think the information is of value

6 Interacting with a journalist and praising them for the articles they are writing or thanking them for a piece they did together

7   Commenting on a friend's post – perhaps someone they worked with many years ago, helping to elevate that person's brand

Here are seven benefits they would get in return:

1   Higher employee retention and recruitment, because people want to work for a company where the leader is connected to the people. Employees don't want to be numbers

2   Loyalty from colleagues, because they feel valued and respected

3   Increased customer/supporter retention and loyalty because they don't feel like numbers either – and it's the start of them becoming brand advocates for your business or organization

4   Better integration with partners, because they see that they are valued within the ecosystem of the business they are partnered with

5   Less flak from influencers because it's hard to be nasty to someone who is nice to you

6   More media opportunities, because journalists are people and they like working with someone who respects and values them

7   Deeper friendships and respect, because friends always appreciate it when their community supports them

If every social CEO had the mindset to do these seven things every week, elevating their community on social media, can you imagine the impact? Can you imagine the change we would see on social platforms? Because when leaders embrace it, just about every manager in their organization would embrace it too – and if that happens, we are talking about a huge, positive impact. That's the power of being a truly social CEO. It starts with you.

If you start your social media journey with this mindset – especially with the Giving Economy first – you will build a strong, credible presence that changes your organization as well as your industry. Praising others and celebrating others is what makes a great leader, and it's central to becoming a social CEO.

Tackling social media cynicism

One of the challenges with social media is that too many people are shouting at us – talking about themselves, their successes, their products or services, them, them, them. This turns people off.

Just because this is how many people behave on social media, we don't have to join the fray. We don't need to participate *like that*. A little bragging is fine, but *only* bragging is totally missing the point.

All deep-thinking leaders tell me that every fibre of their being resists participating in social media in this way. They tell me they're seeing too much nonsense and are struggling to see their social community as authentic or meaningful. It's turning them off participating – the very people we want to be present on social media.

This is a very relevant and ongoing issue with social media. However, when you appreciate that it's about serving your community versus being a megaphone for your opinions, it changes everything.

Feeling cynical or completely disengaged from social media is perfectly understandable, but we must change the rules of what's acceptable and flip it around so we can make sure social media reaches its full and powerful potential. That is all of our jobs today.

We do that by defining our focus (what we want to be known for), then it's about putting that voice into the world – in a powerful, credible, authentic way.

We put our voice into the world by

1 creating our own world-class, highly valuable and relevant content;

2 sharing other's content which inspired something deep within us; and

3 listening to our audience, staying on the pulse of what matters to them and then participating in relevant conversations with them online.

We are now in the Social Age of 'working out loud', but we are also facing a crisis of trust. Our audience is building stronger walls to keep the noise out, and brands – from businesses, charities, government, education, healthcare and more – are struggling to break through to the audiences they want to influence.

It is therefore a time for leaders to step up and become social CEOs – with a mindset of serving their audience, where they are, in a meaningful and authentic way. But you can only achieve this by participating and getting your hands dirty. You can't understand social media if you're not present. You can't gauge its value from outside, looking in.

Only true engagement, where you listen, engage and lead – on the relevant platforms your audience are using – will unlock those insights.

3

Personal branding for CEOs

Tammy Gordon

I will never forget the first time I recognized the power of social media for professional use. It was back in 2007 and I had been robotically tweeting inspirational quotes, statistics and calls to action back to our website. One day, I was present for a conversation with our chief operating officer during which he was complaining that other organizations got more share of media on our issue than we did. What he essentially wanted to know was, 'Why is leader X getting more interviews than we are?'

Back at my desk, I started researching. I looked up each competing organization, who their leaders were – and followed them on Twitter. I went down rabbit holes, looking at who each followed and following the people and organizations that were also relevant to us.

What started out as an 'opposition' research ended up being a revelation in how we used social media for communications and marketing at our organization. Those 'competitors' that I followed were some of the biggest names in the philanthropy space. And what I quickly noticed was that they followed back – and began sharing our content.

It was then that I realized that the power of social media isn't about publishing – it is about connecting and developing relationships with others.

When it comes to your personal use of social media, this is more important than ever. Anyone can publish banal links to your company's press releases, but why is that compelling to follow? As the CEO, you have a unique opportunity to not only lead the messaging for your organization but also develop a unique, multidimensional relationship with your audience.

Overtly developing a 'personal brand' and strategic plan for your social media can often feel heavy-handed for leaders. However, doing so allows you to split the workload with your team, allowing your communications and marketing team to support you, but ensuring that every post on social media under your name is authentic to who you are, and how you would say it.

People follow and connect with leaders for a variety of reasons – product or service affinity, learning about an issue or because you share something in common. As a human, you are more than what you do for a living and your audience may find, follow and enjoy your social media because of something more than just what you do for a living.

When coaching CEOs on how to operationalize their personal brand on social media, we often sketch out a weekly calendar prompt system. For instance, look at the following:

Sample weekly executive social media prompt calendar

Monday: Share a link to an article you read over the weekend that you thought was interesting, with your spin on why it matters.

Tuesday: Give one of your employees a 'shout out' on social media for the great job they are doing.

Wednesday: Follow someone new on social media and start a conversation with them.

Thursday: Share what you are most proud of your company/organization accomplishing this week.

Friday: Share something personal about what you did this week or what you are planning to do this weekend (e.g. cheer on your college team, post a photo from an event you attended, etc.).

The point of these calendar prompts is not that you should only post on those topics on those days. Instead, it's about getting comfortable with thinking about what type of content is appropriate and using social media beyond the basics. Posts can include everything from sharing links, videos and photos to questions, polls and offers.

CEOs that I have worked with report back that these prompts simplified the overwhelming nature of 'what to post and when', taught them more fluidly how to use the platforms, showed them what customers/members were saying about their organization and led to new leads and relationships.

As busy executives, you also need to have a response plan for customer service, media requests and other incoming queries that a more robust and personal social media approach may open you up to. A shared monitoring system with your communications team so that they respond to any asks of you is advised.

One CEO who takes personal branding on social media to the extreme is John Legere of T-Mobile. He is famous for goading competitors with everything from friendly ribbing to outright trolling. His style certainly isn't for everyone or every organization, but breaking down how his personal approach garnered him nearly six million followers on Twitter can give us a few lessons.

Glance at John's accounts on any given day and you'll see a mix of T-Mobile content and calls to action, his family dog, links to amusing articles and maybe even a live-stream of him making his famous #SlowCookerSunday recipes.

Do you have to share this much or this often? No, but approaching your own threshold and balance for what types of content you are comfortable with will allow you a more fluid approach to deciding what and when to post.

Often, a personal approach can be capturing a spontaneous moment with your team and sharing it. Alison Bodor, CEO of the American Frozen Foods Institute, takes a personal approach to content, sharing everything from food safety alerts to membership updates. You may see her posting what she's making her kids for dinner or shopping at the grocery store, but what Alison is doing is creating an online ecosystem that reinforces her organization's brand identity and reflects the culture.

You'll see a theme with the most successful CEOs on social media. They fluidly combine what their business goals and messages are with their own personal voice and narrative of what's happening in their lives. They are purposeful in what they post and ensure that it's said in the way they would say it in person, rather than coming across robotic and 'corporate'.

AARP CEO Jo Ann Jenkins regularly shares her take on issues affecting older Americans on her Twitter account. She even coined the hashtag #DisruptAging to fight against ageist stereotypes online. And while she has a team of talented communicators who support her, Jo Ann ensured early on in her tenure at the organization that she knew how to use the platforms and could post in the moment. That allows her to capture and share photos, whether she's in a NASCAR pit with her Drive to End Hunger initiative or meeting a celebrity at an event. In addition, she has a second monitor on her desk that tracks what people are saying about AARP and the issues she is working on, in real time.

One way to find the right balance of tone, content and cadence might be to follow the CEOs and leaders of brands and organizations that you care about. Study how they blend the personal with the professional and engage with their followers.

Jen Gotch found that getting personal on social media leads to enormous growth – of her company and personally. Her very real Instagram account led her to connect with thousands of individuals and entrepreneurs who were struggling with the balance of leadership and mental health. Today, in addition to running her successful lifestyle brand, ban.do, Jen hosts a podcast called 'Jen Gotch Is OK, Sometimes' on the GirlBoss network and is authoring a book.

For most of my life I have struggled with depression, anxiety, bipolar disorder and ADD. Over the last couple of years I have intentionally used my social media platforms to openly discuss my mental health issues in an effort to remove the stigmas around them and help others feel less alone. This level of vulnerability resonated with my audience on Instagram – and they welcomed and encouraged it enthusiastically. Seeing the positive effect that just even my small influence could have on people was incredibly powerful. So I thought, "How can I incorporate this into my business, ban.do, as well?" – and the Jen Gotch x Iconery collection was created as a natural extension of my efforts. This is a line of necklaces intended to remove the stigmas associated with mental illness and open up conversations. That collection was an impetus for us at ban.do to clarify for ourselves and voice for others what our true values are. We have always focused on being all about fun, but we are also so much more than just fun. We exist to help our customers and community be their best self through encouraging personal and professional betterment. We also strive to help them feel less alone in their struggles by inviting them to be open about those struggles without shame.

We tell our executive clients to think of social media as a cocktail party. If you read your tweet or your Facebook post and it doesn't sound like something you would say, or how you would say it, tweak it to match your personal style. And make sure you are speaking conversationally. You will know it's working when people start talking back to you.

Personal social media, done well, amplifies who you are and what you care about. People who are interested in the things you share and care about will follow and engage with you. And, if you've been authentic with your audience, they are going to be more willing to give you the benefit of the doubt if you find yourself in a crisis.

In the end, it's not about having a million followers. It's about building a direct connection with the right people – the ones who care about the things you care about and who can share your message further.

4

How PR disasters are driving CEOs to embrace social media

Bob Pickard

'Public relations' (PR) means different things to different people. Some say that it is about image or looking good in public. Others suggest that it is more about 'spin control' or media manipulation. There are those who think it is synonymous with getting favourable publicity in the press. More than a few folks feel that PR is synonymous with 'propaganda'. Then there are the executives inside the communications consulting trade – and I am one of them – who think PR should be considered a core strategic management function of the corporation, right up there in importance with finance, HR and marketing.

Many industry studies and academic papers have tackled the task of pegging PR, and the trade associations representing PR agencies have periodically engaged in debates about the definition. For the purposes of this book, we will use the PR term as explained by the

Public Relations and Communications Association in London, who describe it as 'the way organisations communicate with the public, promote themselves, and build a positive reputation and public image'.

Of course, this book is focused on chief executives, who are individuals and not organizations. However, as the leaders of those organizations, CEOs play a conspicuous PR role with a whole constellation of stakeholder constituencies who are interested in their companies. CEOs are highly visible to their own employees, customers, suppliers, partners, regulators and shareholders (especially if publicly traded). There is nothing new about this, and long before the advent of social media, CEOs were often thought of as an organization's premier PR representative and chief spokesperson.

Prior to the omnipresence of smartphones in both private and public places, CEOs spent most of their time operating with a relatively low-profile default posture. Decisions to do high-profile things (e.g. giving a speech, doing a TV interview and making an event appearance) were typically made well in advance and usually in consultation with colleagues. CEOs would communicate carefully crafted long-form content such as speeches or newspaper columns at pre-scheduled intervals. This process was often mapped out in 'PR plans' or 'communications strategies' with tactics plotted on timelines of weeks and months in advance. Such linear PR practices still do occur, but many of them are quickly becoming obsolete as PR becomes less about thinking ahead logically and more about sensing sentiments in the present moment.

CEOs are today just about always within the 'capture radius' of smartphones, so even if they haven't planned any public communication, they are now always potentially 'visible' on social media (which involves both heightened risk of unflattering exposure and increased opportunity for rapid PR deployment). What happens within a CEO's formerly private sphere is now instantly able to be thrust into the glare of the public spotlight. All it takes is someone nearby shooting a video, taking a picture or writing a post. So, CEOs are now usually operating well within 'PR range', and are able – if they want – to communicate easily and openly in short-form spurts with much less logistical preparation required and far less thinking invested. Whether they like it or not, CEOs are 'always on' public figures who are subject to the smartphone surveillance of proximate persons.

In the past, the premium was on careful communication preparation, but now social media creates an inescapable impetus for spontaneous and improvised communication. This modern dynamic means that there is now less time to think, but more pressure to communicate impromptu. The ability to do that well digitally – to communicate online for PR purposes – only comes with experience. While social media is more than a decade old, many CEOs lack mastery of social media techniques because they lack practiced skill using social media themselves. And even then, to know how the technology works is not at all the same thing as knowing how to communicate effectively.

When it comes to social media communication, there is a massive difference between what CEOs are now potentially able to do, what they are actually able to do and what many choose to then do. Some have fully embraced the upside of social media for PR, but even now, most are – or have been at some point – relatively cautious and reluctant, more concerned with the perceived risk of making a career-limiting mistake online. Indeed, CEOs, as a category of people, have been notably hesitant to take up social media for their own communication purposes and use it to its full PR potential.

CEOs are high-status people – we are talking about 'one-percenters' here – who have been raised in a hierarchical world of top-down authority. In the past, communication was telegraphed vertically from the commanding heights of the C-Suite down to a mass audience who were expected to believe what was being explained and were assumed to be passive consumers of controlled information. In this old world, companies could 'buy' PR success and induce the consent of stakeholders. Most CEOs intellectually realize that things have now changed, as ordinary people insist on more horizontal peer-to-peer interactivity with their companies. But that doesn't mean that they actually like what has happened or really want to get on the social media playing field with the public.

Ego and hubris often get in the way of CEO social media adoption; some seem to feel that they didn't need to think much about PR to become a fabulously wealthy executive, so why should they now spend more time worrying about the masses on social media? That describes what I believe is a shrinking minority. There are many inspiring CEO exceptions to such legacy attitudes who are the trailblazers – some of them are authors of chapters in this book.

Looming ever larger is the business challenge posed by digital transformation in the marketplace – many organizations are afraid of being disrupted by AI and emerging new technologies. Unfortunately, many leaders are struggling with this at a time when their organization's very survival may depend on how well they deal with digital imperatives. I believe there is no better PR medium than social media for a leader to dramatically demonstrate a command of digital disruption and in so doing inspire the confidence of stakeholders that an organization has what it takes to stay on top of transformation.

Lately I have seen some CEOs strike an awkward PR pose, saying that their company will be the digitally disruptive leader in their industry 'X' (here in Canada a leading gold producer's CEO stated that his company would be 'the digitally disruptive miner'). Such a key message would be communicated much more credibly and effectively if this particular CEO was on social media, which he isn't.

Over many years of counselling chief executives about their leadership communication, I have reached the firm conclusion that fear is the key to understanding their resistance to using social media as a PR tool (or using it at all because they aren't sure what kind of tool it actually is). Behind that fear is a timidity about taking career risks and a reluctance to humbly admit – in front of others, especially their own employees – the extent of their relative ignorance about something seen to be so fundamentally important as social media.

The good news is that more and more top bosses in the C-Suite are reaching the same conclusion, as former Chrysler CEO Bob Nardelli described in a 2015 blog post which he addressed to his peers: 'No matter your feelings about social media, the fact is that you can't ignore it. Conversations about your company will take place, whether you are a part of them or not. Obviously, it's much better to be involved! For me, the digital age has been intimidating and at times a little embarrassing, but I've tried to move beyond that as I recognize the importance and relevance it plays.'[1]

The understandable tendency among CEOs of not wanting to look 'dumb about digital' in front of their subordinates can manifest in different ways. Some CEOs will be loath to seek the candid counsel they need from their own PR people about how to use social media to communicate. Others will simply delegate all things digital to their CMO, reckoning that social media is merely another sales channel to consumers. The problem with that approach is that many CMOs don't know PR in their bones – if corporate communications reports into them, PR is the junior player – and will see social as being about 'paid' sales, not about 'earned' relationships (the latter properly the province of PR). The transactional sales attitude of marketers to consumers is a much different and less mutual way of thinking than the solicitous professionals of the PR trade who are wired for peer-to-peer two-way communication. PR people are invested in the importance of relationships as the building blocks of social and reputational capital, not just because they want to extract money from a mass audience.

When CEOs do turn to their PR chiefs inside the corporate communications department, some of them – especially long-serving 'flacks' working within the same organization for many years – don't personally possess the requisite social media savvy, meaning that they may not be able to competently or confidently advise the chief executive to become a social CEO. Many are staunch defenders of the old status quo and 'the way we've always done things', which doesn't augur well for social leadership communication.

Inside many organizations, PR doesn't directly report to the CEO. It doesn't even report to the CEO through the adjacent marketing domain. Instead, PR may report to a lawyer-dominated corporate affairs department (which is concerned with compliance more than communication) or even through HR where the executive in charge tends to know little of PR. In such cases, there might actually be a social media superstar working down in corporate communications, but because this is typically a more junior person, in addition to lacking the power of a reporting line to the CEO, s/he may lack the experience and the efficacy required to successfully persuade the company's top boss.

There is an irony here inasmuch as while social media is unmistakably making PR more important, inside many organizations PR tends to remain a subordinate or non-core corporate function. In my decades of experience working inside multinational PR firms, I know that this observation is more apt in describing what happens in some countries compared to others.

Everywhere in the world, to be used most effectively as a PR tool, social media should be properly part of an organization's PR mandate. Because it is the PR people inside the corporation who innately understand how to communicate, they are the ones who should have agency to coach and support the CEO as s/he achieves social media literacy and then, ultimately, PR proficiency.

Let there be no doubt that social media has made PR far more crucial for companies versus past practice. In Canada – and I suspect this is true throughout the English-speaking world – the public strongly agrees. Nanos Research, one of this country's leading pollsters, conducted a study in 2017 asking 1,000 Canadians, 'Do you think that with the rise of social media, PR is becoming more important, less important or as important for organizations today compared to 10 years ago?' Three quarters (76 per cent) said that PR is now 'more important'.

At the same time, study after study has shown that 'communication' is rated as a more important skill for leaders than ever before, and now many people contend that social media is the most important component of communication. John Chambers, the former CEO of Cisco Systems, summarized this well when he stated the following in a 2018 interview: 'Communication is one of the most important skills that a leader and, frankly, most employees now need to excel on the job. You've got to deal with social media, you've got to deal with a dramatically different speed of events, you've got to be able to talk to your shareholders, your employees, your customers and your partners. If you don't have communication skills, you're not going to be an effective leader.'[2]

I reckon that there are still quite a few in the world's C-Suites who haven't grasped that yet. Often the ones who have are the ones who have learned the hard way through the ordeal of crisis communications. 'Crisis' is a lucrative niche domain of PR which has profited from the explosion of issues arising on social media which were previously less publicly sensational before everyone had smartphones (which have been used to reveal/report/chronicle/ sensationalize just about every conceivable form of executive and corporate malfeasance).

While social media has increased spending on crisis communications, a lot of money has been squandered on outmoded strategic thinking (which usually involves stonewalling angry publics on social or issuing old-fashioned 'holding statements' to keep people at bay). Indeed, I am even aware of professional malpractice – unintentional negligence – where some PR pros have harmed a client's interests by advising them to follow communications counsel which was better suited to the mainstream media environment of ten or even twenty years ago compared to today's social media environment.

The result? PR disasters, which in terms of PR agency fees and lost reputation can be staggeringly expensive.

Such avoidable-in-retrospect PR disasters have forced a lot of learning on corporate communications people, and their CEO clients are adapting and learning fast. Here again we see fear as a key factor, where CEOs, afraid of being caught in the middle of dreaded PR disasters, are increasingly compelled to start communicating via social media! This trend has been accelerating because PR disasters have been happening in a famous way almost every day, and they are *all* playing out online on social.

We have seen this pattern happen repeatedly during recent years: when something goes badly wrong for a company in public, all eyes look to its leader. When the CEO is absent from social media or has nothing to say, then an 'information vacuum' occurs, instantly filled by naysayers whose voices become a chorus of condemnation on social media. If companies let that happen, they cede the centre stage of PR to critics, whose collective censure suddenly becomes the new conventional wisdom.

In a crisis communications situation, the online public doesn't just expect to hear an explanation from a CEO but demand it impatiently. Especially if there's some corporate stonewalling at first, the CEO ultimately is almost always forced to say something about what's happened. The beleaguered leader will often try to explain things in an initial statement using a 'corporate speak' that is carefully parsed by legal counsel and, when such inauthentic comments fall flat, outraged online communities start howling for a sincere 'sorry'. Finally, the CEO is forced to come out and offer a proper apology via social media in order for the fury to subside.

Whenever this increasingly predictable cycle occurs, the public spectacle of controversy is invariably labelled as a 'PR disaster'. This term usually means that whatever the facts of the matter are, if a company's CEO fails to communicate convincingly about a crisis – sincerely and in a timely manner on social media – then for sure it must be a PR disaster.

Time after time, this is how crisis communication now plays out, and yet we keep seeing companies making the same mistake over and over again. We saw it in 2017 with United Airlines and in 2018 with Facebook, and there are examples of this in the media almost every day. Today, it is remarkable how many high-profile corporate mistakes are now called 'PR disasters', regardless of whether the corporate PR function is actually disastrous. In most cases, the failure is one of leadership communication: failure by the CEO to attach more importance to corporate communication than to compliance concerns; failure by the CEO to listen to the corporate communicators instead of the corporate lawyers; failure by the CEO to grasp the power of one's own personal communication on social media to shape successful PR outcomes.

The role of the CEO's leadership communication using social media is never more essential than during a crisis. That's because CEOs are real people who personify their brands in an era when companies are expected to communicate like real human people, not like machines or things.

Now, more than ever, the extent to which the CEO is personally involved with the corporate communications effort is one of the strongest predictors of whether a company will experience a PR disaster in the first place.

Specifically, I believe that almost all crisis situations can now be intercepted and successfully addressed with these five elements of social leadership communication:

1 The CEO is present on social media with an active account
   (in their name, but which PR advisers can support), ideally
   on Twitter, as all the journalists are there and because it's the
   social network 'where news happens now'.

2 When the CEO becomes aware of a trending corporate issue
   which could become a crisis, s/he proactively and transparently
   discloses what's happening so that people hear the news first
   from the company's leader (and not from other sources that
   might make it look as if the company was hiding something).

3 The CEO clearly describes what the company is doing about
   the crisis and how he or she feels about the people affected by
   the situation as it develops.

4 If the company has done something wrong, the CEO sincerely
   apologizes and takes leadership responsibility for making
   things right.

5 To ensure that media coverage and social sentiment about
   the unfolding situation are informed and guided by what s/
   he is openly sharing, the CEO provides updates at regular
   intervals, asking for community feedback, setting realistic
   expectations and helpfully pointing people towards resources
   offering information or assistance.

If chief executives communicate authentically in this way on social media as a transparent source of trustworthy information – no weasel words, no spin control – and tune in to the emotional wavelength of their communities with humility, empathy and patience, then they will prevent or quickly solve just about any so-called PR disaster.

For leaders, social media should be about public relationships with stakeholders, custom connectivity, listening with real people, sensing their sentiments, understanding their emotions, channelling their ideas, rallying them to shared purposes. It won't be too long before 'social media savvy' becomes a CEO job requirement, so now is the time to invest resources in social leadership communication.

We have now reached a real turning point where, every day, more and more CEOs have concluded that the risks to their reputation of being *absent* from social media are now greater, for the very first time, than the risks of being *present* on social media. This is why executive communication is now one of the fastest-growing segments of the PR industry worldwide.

Leadership itself is changing in a way that favours the de rigueur adoption of social media for CEO leadership communication. In November 2018, the global executive search firm Russell-Reynolds conducted a study of CEOs and found that

> companies often favour leaders ... with 'loud' personality characteristics such as extroversion, passion and charisma. Our recent analysis of global chief executive role specifications showed that these 'loud' words were used three times more often than those describing 'quiet' characteristics, such as humility, authenticity and listening. These archetypal loud leadership traits have certainly produced great leaders. But the current business climate suggests that they may not be sufficient to make the best leaders for the

future – especially given the increasing volatility, speed of change, disruption and transformation they will have to master. The most effective leaders possess not only the loud traits that allow them to cast big visions and persuade others to follow, but they equally demonstrate the quiet traits that allow them to be vulnerable and connect with others.

These 'leaders of the future' will be social CEOs: listeners as well as talkers, sensors as well as thinkers, literate in technology, fluent in communication and invested in reciprocal relationships of mutual benefit. These are all the same skills demanded of modern PR executives, so the next wave of leaders will probably attach much more importance to the PR function than their predecessors ever did.

5

More than selling: Building social trust with your customers

Chris Bartley

Nobody buys what your company does because of how brilliantly you do it. They buy what they buy because of how well it helps them achieve their aspirations.

Take the example of a pharmaceutical company that spends ten years – and several billion dollars – at the cutting edge of medicine developing a revolutionary gene therapy. Putting yourself in a doctor's shoes, you can probably imagine the magic of discovering something that offers people longer, less compromised lives where previously they had little hope. It's also easy to imagine how quickly that feeling fades to scepticism when a sales representative is standing in front of you selling that same technology. When you are 'sold to' you feel your right to choose freely without any external influence is compromised.

Today we're bombarded with selling messages via email, via social media and on our phones. So we tend to tune out the messages and actively avoid sales people. This in turn makes it more difficult to tell people how your organization can help them with their aspirations.

Growing revenue, a key priority for CEOs, increasingly relies on building a credible voice that customers are open to hearing from. Building organizational social selling excellence is, therefore, critical to ensuring the voices of your sales people carry the authority and trust to be heard among noise of today's promotion-heavy culture.

Perceived authority and authenticity of the 'messenger' drives trust

Rarely do we go out and discover new things on our own without some sort of stimulus prompting it. The reality is that almost everything new we find is the result of indirect, or direct, social selling. This might be a conversation with a peer, an advert, a news story, a sales call, a tweet – or any one of a hundred other sources. Importantly, though, how we perceive that source has a significant impact on what we do next.

For example, a recommendation from a trusted friend might be enough to drive an immediate purchase. An advert or a tweet might only pique someone's interest for a moment, but consensus across multiple interactions amplifies awareness and credibility. This means that if two friends, an ad, several social media posts and a news story all recommend something, the effect on action is amplified significantly.

A study by MINDSPACE found a 1,000 per cent increase in smoking among teenagers when two of their peers smoked, compared to a 26 per cent increase if a parent smoked.[1] This same principle holds true for doctors. Their prescribing behaviour is heavily influenced by what they see their peers endorsing.[2]

The messenger effect, therefore, has an important impact on the speed a prospect progresses through every part of the sales funnel. For example, a 'cold' email from a sales representative generally results in a longer consideration phase than a peer's recommendation on LinkedIn that's been 'liked' by several others. Likewise, a sales person who is not liked, or not fully trusted, by a prospect can prevent a conversion altogether. Finally, the process of the sale, and interactions with any after-sales service, can play a huge role in a customer's future advocacy of a brand.

Build trust, not just more sales channels

Contrary to how it's sometimes presented, social selling is *not* about direct selling via social media. This approach can actually damage the credibility of both the sales person and the brand, with either or both ending up being blocked. Instead, it's more important for sales people to build the credibility of their voice on relevant topics for their audience and industry.

Taken to its ultimate conclusion, social selling is about building a network of peers and advocates, connected to your prospects, who share content that positions the organization's representatives as leading voices on key subjects. Therefore, the objective for your sales teams is building trust in their own personal brands, alongside building trust and awareness of the organization's brand.

Powerful personal brands can become disruptive forces

Nowhere has the concept of building personal brands – linked directly to selling products – been executed better than in cosmetics.

Historically, a small number of long-established beauty brands have totally dominated the cosmetics industry. In 2008 these legacy brands, including Revlon, Maybelline, Rimmel and a few others represented 98 per cent of the market by revenue.[3] Fast forward eleven years and, despite the legacy brands growing at a respectable 4.5 per cent a year – primarily through spending billions on offline and online promotion – they now account for just 60 per cent of the market by revenue.[4]

For these established brands, having lost 40 per cent market share in just eleven years is change on a huge scale. As a comparison, the much-lauded disruptors in the hospitality sector like Airbnb, HomeAway and FlipKey have only been able to take around 10 per cent market share over a similar timespan.[5] What's been achieved by the cosmetics' disruptors, then, is nothing short of revolutionary.

Charlotte Tilbury is an archetypal example. But before diving into the success of Charlotte Tilbury's promotional model, it's vital to understand some cultural insights:

- People under the age of forty-four are three times more likely to say they learn about new products from social media.[6]

- This category of people are influenced more by people they see as 'like them' than they are by brands directly.[7]

- Traditional promotion channels, such as in-store displays, print advertising and television commercials, have less influence on people belonging to this age group.[8]

Those belonging to this age group are a critical audience for the cosmetics industry because, while they only represent 37.9 per cent of byers, they are much quicker to try new products.[9] When asked 'When was the last time you purchased a new cosmetics brand?' 48 per cent of those active in the category replied, 'in the last month'.[10]

This, then, is a group open to new experiences – one that views peers and experts, rather than brands, as more authentic, credible and influential voices. But perhaps most critically, they are highly engaged on social media, particularly visually driven channels like Instagram, Snapchat and YouTube. In fact, the most watched YouTube category for female users is make-up and cosmetics.[11]

When you consider this alongside the fact that over 80 per cent of people say they regularly use YouTube,[12] it makes YouTube the world's most important make-up and beauty channel. This is backed up by the more than 1.5 million beauty videos (accounting for 4.6 billion views) uploaded each month.[13] If you are promoting a cosmetic brand, then YouTube offers access to more of your audience than any other channel.

Before 2013, Charlotte Tilbury wasn't a brand. She was a well-known – and well-connected – UK-based make-up artist. With seed funding from angel investors, she officially launched the Charlotte Tilbury range of cosmetics at Selfridges in London in September 2013. Very quickly it became the retailer's biggest-ever beauty launch. From there brand revenue grew from under £2 million in 2013 to

£75.5 million in 2018, with new stores opening in key locations worldwide.[14]

How did she achieve this astonishing success in such a short time? Behind the success, the launch glitz and the stunning growth lies a social selling approach that typifies the disruptor brands in this sector.

In May 2012, over a year before the much-lauded public launch, the Charlotte Tilbury YouTube channel quietly went live. Its content focused on how to apply make-up and some make-up tips and ways to create different looks. Much more importantly, she complemented this with two of the oldest social selling techniques known to marketing: free samples and word of mouth.

But how Charlotte Tilbury used these techniques was entirely modern. She identified make-up artists who had large numbers of subscribers on their channels but were not household names and sent them her products. Now, it's important to understand that a lot of these 'micro-influencers' had heard of, or already worked with, Charlotte Tilbury the make-up artist. This means that the samples they received were relevant, from a credible known source and therefore likely to get an overwhelmingly positive response. Then word of mouth, via YouTube videos reviewing the products, did the rest.

Building awareness and credibility with a significant number of prospects pre-launch accelerated the consideration phase of her sales funnel, resulting in record-breaking sales at launch. This strategy continues to propel growth to this day. Charlotte Tilbury is not simply pushing a product: she's showing leadership, expertise and authenticity – and is supporting people who aspire to look like her clients through her products.

The key tool for the next generation of B2B sales

The value of creating powerful personal brands translates directly into business-to-business (B2B) selling. In healthcare, for example, the extraordinary sales person of five years ago is often the ordinary sales person of today. Their audience – doctors – has changed so fast that the skillsets that drove past successes are holding traditional healthcare salespeople back today.

What's changed? Today, 86 per cent of doctors use their phones, tablets and laptops daily to access information relevant to their clinical practice.[15] Many of them use their phones during the work day, and even during consultations with patients, to look up medical information.[16] A raft of specialist online sources and apps provide access to clinical tools, news, research and case studies instantly.

In the past, the primary source of much of this information was regular meetings with sales reps who generally presented just their companies' data. Today, however, face-to-face sales rep access to doctors has fallen to just 46 per cent and call times average less than three minutes.[17] Sales people who still rely on face-to-face interactions, where they directly promote their products, are struggling to even get in the doctor's office door.

Today's best healthcare sales people are carefully building their personal brands from the perspective of how it adds value to digitally savvy doctors. They are becoming curators of relevant content, providing a filter for news, research, events and opinions that are relevant to the specific needs of the doctors in that field. In some cases, this content is shared directly via email, or via messenger tools like WhatsApp, and in other situations via LinkedIn and Twitter.

The aim is to be seen as highly informed about the absolute latest developments in a specific area of medicine. Additionally, building a network of connections around the globe through social media allows these sales people to see what is being shared by other doctors and experts. This is critical. Knowing that Dr Jones, a world leader in a specific area of medicine, but who's based in Australia, has just shared some thoughts about a new study, or being able to provide a summary of a WebEx session by Dr Smith from a recent conference in Spain, offers doctors value they find hard to get elsewhere.

The objective of this activity is never to be overtly promotional. It's to build credibility and visibility and provide value to the audience. The result of a strong personal brand is greater access, more call opportunities, permission to share content directly – and in some cases, direct advocacy of the content by doctors to their peers.

This approach and these customer trends are not limited to healthcare. They apply to almost every industry and type of business-to-business selling.

Organizational excellence in social selling excellence: A priority for CEOs

In today's world, direct selling has become increasingly difficult. People are far less inclined to give brands – or their salespeople – their attention and time. Regardless of the industry, potential customers will only engage with those who they perceive as having the credibility and expertise to help them achieve their desired outcomes.

Being relevant and successful in this context means ensuring sales teams build credible personal brands and use social selling to expand the reach of their message beyond just the people they can directly access in a day. Doing so is vital to enabling brands and their salespeople to appeal to – and build affinity with – modern buyers, helping them stay open to seeing how your brand can help them achieve their aspirations.

Three steps to more effective social selling

If you're a CEO looking to improve or maintain your company's growth, then ensuring understanding and adoption of these three social selling principles throughout your organization should be a key priority:

- Social media is a way for sales people to build the credibility and visibility of their voice on relevant topics with your audience. They should focus on building a network of connections who are also connected to sales prospects and who share content that helps position the company's representatives as visible, credible and well informed.

- Sales people with a greater level of recognition and trust benefit from increased access and share of voice. Having permission to engage prospects more deeply gives them the opportunity to better demonstrate how the brands

they promote will support the customer in achieving their
aspirations.

- Strong personal brands can create a halo effect for a company's
  products, resulting in happier customers, greater brand
  advocacy, better reviews and accelerated movement of
  potential customers from awareness to purchase.

6

How social media can bring talent and opportunity to your door

Nicola Brentnall

This chapter looks at how CEOs are using social media to attract talent to their organizations.

Just the suggestion of doing this may leave some readers nonplussed, but I hope that by the end of this chapter, anyone who wasn't convinced will be firing up Twitter and Instagram for the first time and jumping in – for a whole world of new connections and talented collaborators awaits you in social media land.

Let's get to it.

For me, the clue to all this can be found in this definition of social media: 'the collective of online communications channels dedicated to community-based input, interaction, content-sharing and collaboration'[1]. With collaboration being an essential part.

Here are a few statistics to get us going.

The world is connected. Of the 7 billion people around today, there are 5 billion mobile phone users, 4 billion internet users and 2.5 billion smartphone users. Social media has a global reach – over 2 billion Facebook users, 1.5 billion YouTube users, 1 billion people on Instagram and over 300,000 Twitter users. Connection will continue to grow. Global smartphone adoption will be 80 per cent by 2025 and, by the same year, another 1.6 billion users will have come online.[2]

A digital organization

The Queen's Commonwealth Trust (QCT) is a digital organization that lives in this modern, connected world. We champion, fund and connect young leaders who are working hard to change the world. We share their stories, give them a platform to amplify their ideas and inspire others to join in. We can only build a connected, global collaboration of talented young people if we do it online – and this is only possible through the power of social media.

As the CEO of QCT, I have to be seen to be leading by example, connecting with young people around the world in an accessible way. My social channel *du jour* is Twitter, but QCT works across Instagram, LinkedIn and Facebook – we place our messages and news of our work in the places young people go.

And of course, millennials shop social. They check everything out online first. It informs the decisions they make, what they buy, where they choose to work and what news they read. They know that the fastest way to mobilize support to their causes or campaigns is to do it online. They work with those they find there, those who respond to them – and they get stuff done.

Take, for example, the hashtag #AMarchforOurLives. The organizers were mostly students from Marjorie Stoneman Douglas School in Parkland, Florida, where seventeen people died from gunshot wounds on 14 February 2018. Having lost friends, these young people wanted to see a change to gun control laws in the United States. They used social media as oxygen to fan the flames of their cause. Through a burning desire for change, they used the power of a hashtag to bring people together. They built followers on social media and networks around the United States at astonishing volume and pace. This has helped to stimulate a massive increase in voter registrations to vote in candidates in support of gun control. At the time of writing, two dozen candidates for Congress that received National Rifle Association backing were defeated at the polls – in no small part due to their efforts. While a very long road is ahead, it is possible that these students are going to drive a change in the law.

More recently, #FridaysForFuture is bringing millions of schoolchildren together and out on strike, marching for a radical change in approach to tackling the climate crisis. This is what harnessing the power of social media can do. Just imagine how something like this, even on a fraction of the scale, could transform the cause or organization *you* are passionate about.

Adam Bradford, Founder of Adam Bradford Associates, an advisor to young entrepreneurs worldwide and to The Queen's Commonwealth Trust, agrees thus:

Young people are increasingly using social media to build vast personal and professional networks. Through my own social media channels in recent years I have accessed thousands of other young people like me, working in the social impact space from all corners of the earth. From Vanuatu to Venezuela, Saint Lucia to South Africa, I have made friends for life and colleagues sometimes even out of just a single tweet. This new movement is exciting, and it is something I find incredibly special and affirming for the sector, the way we can unite to solve the world's biggest challenges with the aid of technology.

Showing up is everything

So, for those of us working with the younger generation, social is the world in which participation is all. For us, as CEOs, as our audience would say, showing up is everything.

Young people engage when they find authenticity, transparency, honesty, responsiveness – in the brands they follow and in the leaders that represent them. This means that CEOs need to be actively engaged in an authentic dialogue with them. My advice is 'Do not delegate this'. Young people want to see you and understand what you stand for. Tread with care though, as Trey Kennedy brilliantly observed in this tweet, real perils await if you try too hard to relate: https://twitter .com/TreyNKennedy/status/1061358800601604098.

Your social activity should also fit with your organization's overall social media strategy. This should cover tone of voice, design, what you comment on – and when – across the various channels you use. Share the lessons you learn as a leader and the direction your organization is taking. Be open about challenges and mess-ups, as well as share the success stories. Bring your values and culture to life and you will find more people following your work, liking your posts, seeking information about your organization, wanting to get involved in some way.

At QCT, we know that young people find the visibility and accessibility to me as CEO on social media to be a great feature of the operation. This is one of the reasons why they want to engage with us.

This draws other talent to our channels, as Adam Bradford illustrates in how we came to know each other:

> I met Nicola via a series of tweets, and that connection and the 'virtual coffee' we have every time we tweet allows Nicola to get a micro glimpse into what I'm working on, my thoughts and my impact – all in a few seconds. The same can be said for me; not only does Nicola get to learn about where I'm at, but I also uniquely get to exchange and check in with her at the same time. Now, I can tweet or post on Facebook that I'm travelling to a particular country for a project and I will have hundreds of young people and organizations offering hospitality and opening their arms to let us all collaborate.

I am conscious of the paradox, of course. In his article 'The (Continuing) Enigma of Kaspar Hauser'[3] Andrew Millner describes this well: 'how youth organizations are run by middle-aged people who all too often fail to involve youth voices in the development of their work, talking at them, not with them'.

Checks appearance in the mirror. Sighs. Youth and me parted company a long time ago, but given the purpose of QCT, there is no 'talking at' here, because the *whole* point is to connect with young people, to share their talent, advice and insights with others. We are posting loads of contributions from young people – and this will attract more interest and talent to this work. Our other supporters love the idea of social media and are beginning to share their skills with young people through it.

We are not the only ones. Caroline Price, Director of Services for Beat Eating Disorders and the Social CEOs Best Leader on Social Media 2018 (so she should know!), is in no doubt about the usefulness of social media to get ideas, volunteers and staff to help grow and develop her organization:

> We have clinical associate trainers and digital volunteers that heard about the roles through my Twitter feed, and some have seen it through LinkedIn too. I always check social to look up organizations we might partner with. It gives a good sense of the type of organization it is, its values and how it relates to its beneficiaries.

This is all just so much common sense, right? Wrong.

There are way too many examples on social media where questions are being asked about young people, or statements being made about their views, attitudes or participation – without knowledge of the reality or consulting or engaging with them. So many opportunities to gain trust, engagement and talent are lost as a result.

What follows is a description of real events. Only the names have been changed to protect the innocent.

Event A took place in 2018. The theme was 'collaboration to effect change'. It aimed for a suitably youthful vibe. One thousand delegates packed into the venue, mostly from the social purpose sector. Now, anyone entering the 'youthful change' world needs to know and understand young people involved in this work – who they follow, when they meet, what they do. Because that way you can do great things like, well, collaborate with fresh talent so your organization is able to effect change more effectively. Strange, that.

Social media was an active part of the publicity for Event A, which was good. Twitter, as Twitter does, covered comments from delegates that suggested there was 'millennial bashing' going on, with claims at this event that millennials are not giving, engaging or remaining committed to social purpose work.

Meanwhile, literally just up the road from Event A, 1,800 young people, mostly millennials, were gathered for Event B. Social media was awash with Event B. It was covered on many local news channels.

Event B was all about social purpose work and millennials' desire and drive for meaningful change on issues they care about – and the steps, collaboration and action they take to get stuff done. Young founders of social purpose organizations – many started with nothing but passion – were speaking about what they achieved. Multinationals sponsor this event and send delegates from all over the world. Big names turn out in full force to support the serious messages it shares – the type of big corporates with their large CSR budgets that Event A could only dream of, and pretty much right next door. Support, financial and otherwise, was forthcoming for the speakers on stage. Collaborations were struck, and partnerships to effect change across the world were forged.

Meanwhile, over at Event A, no one noticed this. Awkward! Opportunities were surely lost here – and all that could have subsequently happened just never came to light.

Don't just take my word for it. Jessica Dewhurst, founder of The Justice Desk and a collaborator with QCT, shared these thoughts:

> Our training coordinator found our Twitter account online and messaged us asking how he could get involved. We then sent him some more information on us, which resulted in him engaging with us online more. Eventually, when we posted that a position was available, he was one of the first to apply. The same goes for our social media manager who contacted us saying that she loved our social media but, if given the chance, she could do it better. We gave her the challenge and she was right. Other organizations have retweeted or shared our posts (and vice-versa) which have resulted in us in-boxing and organising face to face meetings. Organizations we didn't even know existed started reaching out, and now we have some really solid partnerships with them.

If you don't know The Justice Desk, what this means is that more of the world's most vulnerable children have access to support and safety. Pretty important stuff – secured because Jessica shows up on social all the time.

One last shout-out to get social, CEOs.

I met Jenny Hodgson of the Global Community Foundations network on social media, through the #ShiftThePower hashtag. Jenny's work is making sure the imbalance of power in grant-making is addressed, driving to put philanthropy decisions in the hands of local people. This is right up my street – prioritizing local insight, expertise and experience and sharing it widely with others. Through Jenny I have been introduced to like-minded people in philanthropy around the world and I am learning a huge amount from them.

One such person is Barbara Nöst, Director of the Zambian Governance Foundation, a leader I met for a happy breakfast in Lusaka in November 2018. As we were sharing stories of our work, she explained how she wanted to work with local radio to support civil society organizations campaigning to protect the Luangwa, one of the last free-flowing rivers in Zambia – but was struggling to make progress.

Now, for those of us unfamiliar with this issue – trust me – this is a big deal. The Luangwa is home to some of the largest concentrations of elephants, hippos, rhinos and buffalo herds in the world, and to over 400 species of birds. This abundant wildlife supports a booming tourism industry; the river is also a vital lifeline to the many small farming communities along its banks. The Luangwa, however, now faces many threats, including deforestation and, worst of all, a proposed dam at Ndevu Gorge which would transform the river and put all those who depend on it at risk.[4]

I introduced Barbara to Brighton Kaoma, a social CEO, a partner of QCT and the founder of The Agents of Change Foundation, an organization that trains young people to be radio journalists across Zambia. Brighton has a network of them, all broadcasting regularly to the heart of their local communities every week, bringing attention to social causes they care about and mobilizing their listeners to take action. Their big passions are conservation and climate change.

This conversation meant Barbara could have an army of talent connecting to this cause. Maybe, just maybe, like #AMarchForOurLives, these activists could be the deciding factor that will #KeepTheLuangawaFlowing. Time will tell.

Returning the favour, Barbara introduced me to Likumbi Kapihya, the manager of the Social Enterprise Academy in Zambia. Likumbi helps deliver courses to young people who are keen to set up their own social purpose businesses. Funding streams are available for those who have got underway, but too many young people cannot even start as they don't have the money to pay the initial course fees. These courses maximize the chance of success and hook young people into a network of support. The fees are very small, but if money is tight and the choice is feeding the family or going on a course, poverty decides the priority, no matter what.

What if QCT or funders like it could offer tiny grants to help these young people leap over the fees issue, join the courses and get going? This would allow a river of talent to flow freely, just like the Luangwa, bringing sustainable income to families and communities alike. In turn, these entrepreneurs will inspire others to get started. It is early days, but if this happens at QCT, then it would be fair to say that #ShiftThePower paved the way.

Social media does this stuff. It closes the gap; it joins the dots. It draws people together who might never otherwise meet, often from opposite sides of the world, who in turn make great things happen. But for this to work, you have to be there.

Showing up is everything. Join us.

7

Internal engagement

Euan Semple

Changing expectations

The consumerization of technology is having a profound effect on how we see ourselves, both individually and collectively. We now have the power in our hands to access just about any information instantly.

Our ability to share our insights and opinions with lightning speed across organizational, political and geographical boundaries has never been seen before. We are still not quite sure what to do with it. But this is not just a technological revolution; it is a social change at the same time, one supporting the other.

'Hyperlinks subvert hierarchies,' as David Weinberger once wrote – and the full ongoing consequences of this are still to become apparent.

Digital transformation

When people talk of digital transformation, they are often unclear about the meaning of the word 'digital' – and rarely consider the scope of true transformation.

Digital is a distancing word. It allows people to think, 'Oh, we have people who do digital'. But true digital transformation involves the whole organization. It is as much about culture and managerial behaviour as it is about technology.

In fact, when asked for my view on what digital transformation means, I say that it is our response to the fact that your staff and your customers are finding their voices online. Initially they are using the tools to talk to each other, but increasingly they are able to connect between the two groups.

Most businesses and organizations have no idea how to deal with this. Most managers are still uncomfortable engaging online, and senior leadership struggle to define their role in this increasingly volatile connected world. We devolve the challenge to communications or marketing departments, but even PR and marketing firms regularly get things wrong, and the consequences can be brutal.

So, part of the responsibility of the social CEO in the modern digitally enabled world is to proactively embrace these opportunities, face these challenges and lead the way into new ways of working.

The opportunity

The true impact of digital transformation lies in thinking about our organizations in a radically different way. We will still have hierarchies, and control will still rest with the middle and the top, but alongside this conventional structure there has always been the 'real' organization: powerful networks of smart people who trust each other and who connect to get the work done.

These networks can now flourish and, thanks to the new online tools, we can now see and engage with them. Once you have flourishing internal social networks, and tools like blogs, the age-old challenge of 'we don't know what we know' begins to diminish. You can see the conversations taking place that would previously have happened around the water cooler. You can see where tensions are rising before they become a problem. You can see who the smart people in your business are – and they may not all be the ones with the fancy job titles.

This is a drive towards decentralization, distributed trust and collective responsibility. The results of this, if fully embraced, can be increased speed and reduced costs. But it takes courage to embrace these opportunities and skill to know how to do so.

The other shift that we see taking place is one towards an apparently more complex world. This can initially be intimidating, and it is certainly disruptive. But the world has always been complex; we have just hidden this fact behind a veneer of order.

When people express the fear that social media means a loss of control, I counter this with the argument that they have never had control. They have had the *appearance* of control; they owned the channels, they had the authority, but if no one read their memos or forty-page reports, then they had no control whatsoever.

In contrast, becoming good at using social tools offers the prospect of gaining influence over increasingly large and powerful networks. This is how to replace control. Influence the key people in your organization through gaining their trust and increasing your credibility. Taking risks and being seen to be brave. These are counter-intuitive behaviours for many current managers, and they will need help and leadership in their attempts to adopt them.

Digital leadership

These changes call for a different approach to management and leadership. It calls for greater engagement and greater transparency. People increasingly expect those they work with to have an online presence and to be active in those networks that we increasingly use to determine who is trustworthy and who is not.

Failing to appear on a Google search for your name will make people think twice about your credibility, and the first thing most people do when they encounter someone new at work is look up their LinkedIn profile. Making sure that you are visible online and that you are happy with what is visible are increasingly important competencies.

People are also becoming more comfortable with online communications. Clearly the tools need to be appropriate to the job, and you still hear horror stories of people's work contract being terminated by text, but not every interaction needs to be face-to-face or on the phone. Some communication is better handled in an asynchronous and recordable way online. The art of crafting a well-written tweet is like writing a Japanese haiku. You only get so many words, or so much space, and concision is a key skill. Sadly, much business writing is verbose and opaque.

Words, words, words

Not everyone finds it easy to write. We all have hang-ups from our school days about what good writing is, and this nervousness is often exacerbated in the workplace, where an ability to turn out bland 'management boilerplate-speak' is seen to be a primary skill.

It often surprises me how difficult people – sometimes quite senior people – find it to say clearly what they mean in plain language. There is an understandable nervous reaction to saying difficult things that causes us to obscure them in third person, complex language. But the tone of the internet is direct and personal. Being able to speak like this with confidence is a key skill of the social CEO. In the early days of blogging, we used to refer to this as 'finding your voice', and it is still an essential characteristic of online writing and the ability to build trust and relationships.

Why it is worth it

The paybacks of developing the confidence to say what you think online can be huge. Being able to directly connect with people in your organization, without mediation by middle layers of management, can be very attractive to chief executives.

Even if it is just listening to what people are saying, there is a huge advantage to be gained from this first-hand connection. Then, if something is worth responding to, the ability to do so directly can be very influential. Many staff – and customers for that matter – just want to be heard. Their expectations are surprisingly low. More often than not they don't expect you to change the world; they just want you to understand their perspectives.

Social networks give you the ability to do this on a grand scale. A prime example of this is Gary Turner, the Managing Director of

Xero, the online accounting firm, who is a master at using social networks, both internal and external, popping up to join in when appropriate.

One of my favourite examples of this was when a couple of his customers were chatting about Xero on Twitter. Because he followed the #Xero hashtag, Gary was able to see this conversation taking place. When the two customers began to arrange to have a coffee together to discuss their accounting, Gary popped up to ask if it would be fine if he joined them.

The customers were blown away by the fact that not only was Gary listening to their concerns but he was also prepared to join in and engage in the conversation directly and in person. This situation was 1,000,000 miles away from the orchestrated PR and marketing attempts to achieve the same end. This was direct, authentic and, for Gary, fun.

Another great example of the benefits of online conversations, this time internal, is Stephen Quest, Director General for Tax and Customs, at the European Commission. Stephen began blogging a number of years ago and has lots of valuable experience of the challenges and benefits of opening up to an internal audience.

He tells great stories of the benefits that 'thinking out loud' brought: greater visibility, people offering to solve problems, reduced confusion in meetings. When Stephen asked me to run a workshop at the commission for his peers, we both expected about twenty people. Ninety turned up and we had to move to a bigger room! They had obviously been watching what Stephen was doing and how well it was working for him.

Challenging times ahead

But there are challenges coming too. Much is made these days of the power of automation and artificial intelligence. Until now it has principally been blue-collar jobs that have been affected by robotics and advanced systems, but the next group to be affected will be the white-collar, knowledge work jobs that are the norm in so many organizations.

There is even the prospect of management being replaced by technology! We are all becoming increasingly used to interacting with even basic AI in the form of Alexa or Siri and are learning to accommodate their foibles in order to get quick and easy access to functionality.

At the same time, chatbots are becoming more and more sophisticated and are increasingly being used to answer questions in the context of HR and Learning and Development. These chatbots are even able to adjust their language to the demographics of the person they are talking to, and their ability to navigate through lots of information on the basis of interactions with you are improving apace.

At a conference in Sydney on the workplace of the future, I slightly mischievously asked the audience of sixty people whether, if they had clear objectives and KPIs, they would prefer to interact with a chatbot on a daily basis rather than their current line manager. More than half the room put their hands up!

So, in the face of this ongoing march of automation, the way to stay ahead of the robots is to rediscover the human characteristics that we have tended to keep hidden in the interests of apparent stability and predictability. Rather than keeping our heads down, being safe and not rocking the boat (if that is all you do, I have a bot that can do it cheaper) we are going to have to discover our voice, think harder, share better – and be braver.

The risks

In my own book, *Organizations Don't Tweet, People Do*, I compare watching someone senior, perhaps bullied into using social media by the communications department, as a bit like watching your dad dancing at the disco. You're proud of him for having a go, but rather wish he would sit down!

Clearly there are risks involved in any new way of behaving in your organization. I mentioned authenticity earlier in this chapter. Undoubtedly if you find it difficult to find your voice and be authentic, it may be better not to get involved.

Having said that, the bigger risk is being absent. It will be increasingly obvious who engages and who doesn't. You may even be called upon to justify your lack of engagement. Not being across the fast-moving and complex world that will increasingly be your organization will also bring with it its own risks. Not having a finger on the pulse will have consequences.

We have all seen on the internet how things can quickly run out of control. Not realizing this, and not having a basis on which to respond quickly enough, represents a significant risk.

Many organizations are attempting to be 2.0 outside when they're not even 1.0 inside. Their ability to get their act straight when the shit hits the fan is compromised by their slow-moving and bureaucratic internal systems. Working out who, and how, should respond to external conversations that may be threatening your organization's reputation needs to be done quickly and effectively. If you are able to understand this medium and the way it works, you are far better placed to ensure that your organization has the right systems and behaviours to be able to make this happen.

Showing the way

Modelling new behaviours is the most effective way of getting them more widely adopted. Senior leadership using social tools confidently and to good effect signals their effectiveness and encourages more widespread adoption. It also helps to spread and extend the network.

If the only people using social tools are those at lower levels, or those who don't have access to more traditional communications, then your ecosystem will be skewed to a particular demographic. The real benefit of social networks in a business comes when they represent the broad scope of types of people and roles that it takes to make a modern organization function. Indeed, when you get the right mix of creative types, people who prefer structure, those who are confident and vocal and those whose voices are traditionally quieter, then you will see that the ecosystems that make your organization tick start to work on their own.

In fact, this is the ultimate payback of taking the risk of being a social CEO. Nature is full of self-organizing systems, and humans are capable of the same. And yet we get in our own way with rules and structures, dogma and ideology. Once you learn to trust your people – and yes, of course deal with the miscreants and outliers – then you will find that things that currently take up much of your time and effort will start to drop away. Opportunities will emerge quicker and not be missed. Threats will be spotted and dealt with faster and more effectively. Staff will feel more engaged and management will feel less beleaguered. Sounds too good to be true? Why not give it a go and see?

Five tips for making this work

1   Go for it and engage fully in online conversations.

2   Become obsessively interested in the conversations that are taking place both inside your organization and outside on the web.

3   Learn to discern the difference between signal and noise.

4   Be ruthless in managing your time online and get better at making sure the return on investment (ROI) stacks up for you personally.

5   Spread the word and become an evangelist for this new and empowering way of working.

8

Social leadership in small and medium businesses

David Taylor

We now live in a fast-paced digital world where all business leaders, regardless of the size of their organization, need to stay abreast of technological developments and have the communication skills to engage with both customers and staff.

In large organizations, the management team or C-Suite usually has the luxury of a marketing and/or PR team to handle communications and to control any social media campaigns. However, as many of my fellow writers will attest elsewhere in this book, even big business needs social leaders. The key issue in corporations, though, is that too many executives still think they can delegate social processes to their staff and not get involved themselves.

Those running small- and medium-sized businesses (SMBs), on the other hand, don't have the luxury of communications teams and indeed may still be hands-on with a multitude of tasks, from IT to HR and finance to marketing.

Ask many older SMB owners and they will baulk at the idea of being 'social leaders'. Many will complain that they 'don't have the time', or 'it's not business-critical'. Others will say that they can't immediately identify the return on investment (ROI) from using social media. Yet there are so many advantages to using social media for forward-thinking SMB owners. From thought leadership to business intelligence, there are a myriad of ways that even the most time-poor business leaders can harness the power of social.

I will throw in a note of caution here though: any activity MUST be done as part of your company's overall digital engagement strategy or else it simply becomes a wasteful distraction.

Benefits

Let's now look at the benefits of being an SMB social leader.

As the owner of your business, you are the ultimate *brand ambassador*. You should therefore be leading from the front by staying visible at networking events and also online using, at the very least, your LinkedIn profile as a de facto personal, professional website. If you don't feel comfortable posting online, then at the very least share any content being generated by your company, whether this be press releases, reports or simply a strong image.

Simon Morris, Director at GCW, a company specializing in developing town centres, says this:

It feels a brave step to share your opinions with the world and lay yourself open to criticism and challenge. But as leaders, that's what we must do in order to differentiate ourselves and our businesses from the competition. Commentary, original content and opinions must be done within the digital strategy of the business to ensure continuity of message and therefore achieve the greatest impact.

For those of you who are a little more confident and are happy to air their views about their industry or profession, social media enables you to become a *thought leader*. Whether you are tweeting your company's blog posts or writing articles on LinkedIn, you can start to become a real influencer. And if you are comfortable in front of the camera, you may even want to start creating regular vlogs. John Dixon, the Managing Director of video skills training company Brightest Bulb, makes full use of his film-making knowledge to grow his own brand on LinkedIn. He says, 'Today's CEO should view video production within their business as a core competency, alongside other disciplines, such as Excel or Power Point, which were once viewed as the domain of experts.'

Staying abreast of the latest trends, monitoring your competitors and keeping in touch with your clients can all be very time-consuming, yet are all important elements in building useful *business intelligence*. Through Twitter lists or connecting with the right people on LinkedIn, it is perfectly possible to gain the necessary insights you need quickly and simply.

Ian Purvis, the Managing Director of Porterfield PR, says,

For a number of years now I've been using social media as a way to engage directly with the key journalists and publications relating to the commercial property industry. Twitter in particular has been a fantastic way for me to stay up-to-date with all the latest news, what's happening with my clients and also what my competitors are up to. In terms of LinkedIn, this is also a valuable source of information for me, as well as being a useful CRM (customer relationship management) system.

Small businesses, just like large ones, crave the spotlight and are always looking for new ways to improve their profile with journalists and other key influencers. Social media is a fantastic *PR tool*.

David Gordon, Principal Solicitor at DG Law, comments, 'Social media has been an enormous benefit to my business. It's allowed me to develop a profile which previously I would have had to rely on PR agents and expensive advertorials for. It allows me and the practice to be seen in places which we wouldn't normally reach. It can also help with networking to key influencers and potential clients.'

One area of social media overlooked by many small business owners is *recruitment*. LinkedIn was originally set up as a recruitment platform and is still an inexpensive way of finding new talent to hire. Facebook and even Instagram are now also viable ways of growing your company's brand and attracting the right staff. Insurance company Lexham recently took the decision to start recruiting using Facebook ads, successfully hiring two new members of staff and saving money on fees.

As well as attracting potential employees, social media can also be the perfect way to reach out to *potential investors*, whether through crowdfunding or finding angel investors.

Laurence Taylor, Founder and Chair of bookkeeping start-up Easy As 123, says,

> In our situation as a software/service startup with not many barriers to entry, one key question was about how widely we would cast our net, just in case anybody felt minded to steal our business model! Instead of going for an established crowdfunding platform with lots of unknown people signed up as potential investors, we decided to create a microsite on our website and then invite specific interested parties onto it. These people were sometimes already known to us, but most often we were able to target new people by either going through the LinkedIn profiles of existing contacts and connecting via a personal invitation or using LinkedIn Sales Navigator. The latter is an extremely useful tool that allows you to filter profiles by tags and find people who are interested specifically in your sector.

As a leader, you need to be working your *network* of connections. Anita Johnson, Managing Director of Leatfield Ltd, agrees:

> I've found social media to be an invaluable tool for building relationships and creating genuine interest and conversations regarding our offering. In an environment where business owners are so pushed for time, social media creates a really good opportunity to connect with and support our target audience, who are business owners. We planned from day one to have a strong social media presence and it's been worthwhile investing both time and money in creating this. If you think you can avoid it in your future strategy, my personal opinion is that you'll regret it!

Finally, let's not forget that social media can be used internally as well as externally.

Even inside small businesses, it is important to keep *internal communications* simple, quick, mobile and designed around the needs of your staff. From WhatsApp groups and Facebook Messenger to Yammer or Google Hangouts, there are a range of options for you to use.

Building social media into your business life

As already mentioned, having no focus for social media will generally mean you waste time and energy. There is also an opportunity cost of not concentrating on other areas of your business. So, in order to make the best use of your resources, you need to have a proper digital engagement plan in place – not just for your business but also for you, personally.

Here are six simple steps you can take in order to put such a plan together:

Step one: Understand what specific business goals will be achieved through you being active on social media. You can choose any of the eight suggestions mentioned above or you may indeed identify others, such as lead conversion, sales or marketing.

Step two: Think about being an innovator and encouraging those within your business to put their heads above the parapet. Fortunately, many start-ups and SMBs are not constricted by corporate dogma in the same way that larger businesses often are, so they have the flexibility and opportunity to incubate new ideas. You will also need to lead from the front and really encourage as many people within your business to 'get social' too. Incentivize staff to contribute content, put together proactive social media guidelines and ensure those who are online are 'brand aligned'.

Step three: You are what you tweet/post/upload. You therefore need enough quality content to be able to engage your various stakeholder audiences over days, weeks, months and even years. That content doesn't necessarily have to come from you, but as the boss or senior manager, you need to be willing to do your bit.

Step four: Social media is about being, well ... social! That means listening and engaging as well as posting. Even if you have someone employed as a community/social media manager – and this could even be outsourced – you need to be active yourself. Whether you post regularly, engage with your LinkedIn connections or join hashtag conversations on Twitter, it is important that you act like a truly social leader.

Step five: Social networks are now giant targeted advertising platforms. As a business owner you have the opportunity to buy space on them to reach potentially vast new audiences. Facebook advertising, YouTube AdWords and LinkedIn Sponsored Content all offer even those businesses with the most meagre of advertising budgets cost-effective opportunities.

Step six: As well as being targeted ad platforms, social networks are also data centres. From monitoring hashtags to building sales funnels via LinkedIn Sales Navigator, you have access to large amounts of valuable data which you can use for business intelligence. And on a personal level, if you decide to have a Twitter account, creating lists will help you stay on top of the information important to you as a leader.

The challenge

Clearly all of these activities are time-consuming and may involve you changing decades-long working practices – and here's where the key challenge lies. Many business owners who are in their late forties onwards really struggle to make the most of technology – and men in particular are often the culprits here. Pride, stubbornness, fear of technology and laziness are all reasons why thousands of business owners can't or won't adapt to new ways of working.

Furthermore, as the boss or one of the senior management team, you really don't want to come across as ignorant about modern working methods and technology. In fact, a refusal to change could spell danger for your business.

A simple way to dip your toe in the water is simply to monitor what your peers are doing online – you may be very surprised by what you find. You can easily set up an unbranded/anonymous Twitter account and just listen to what people in your industry are saying. Alternatively you can set your profile on LinkedIn to private and look up your competitors, business partners or clients in the search bar to see what they are doing on the site.

Also, if you have millennials (those aged under about thirty-five) in your business, work with them so they can reverse-mentor you. These are digital natives who have grown up with websites, instant messaging and social media, so they are well positioned to help you thrive in this new world. Some of them could even go on to become digital champions within your business.

Five top tips to take away

1　Ensure your business is digitally savvy and that you have some form of digital engagement strategy in place.

2　If you have to pick just one social media channel, make the most of LinkedIn. Master this and you can then think about using Twitter.

3　If you do want to dip your toe in Twitter, use it as a newsfeed first without engaging.

4　Think about what you need to do to become a thought leader. What have you got to say, what issues do you want to talk about and how could you represent your company as a brand ambassador?

5　Learn from those around you – even the youngest members of your team.

9

Why charity CEOs need to be on social media

Zoe Amar

Hundreds of years from now, when historians look back at our time, they will talk about how social media changed our society. It's our main source of information, from breaking news and recipes to health conditions and politics. And it's where we promote ourselves most – just witness the countless business leaders and politicians making the headlines as a result of their social media activity. Social media is increasingly where we define ourselves and find our place in the world.

Smart politicians and leaders have always known this. At the time of writing this chapter, 89 per cent of UK MPs are on Twitter.[1] Donald Trump is adept at using Twitter to control the news cycle. Elon Musk seems hooked on using Twitter to tell us about his day and plans for his companies – for better or worse. And charity CEOs are becoming more visible on social media, using these channels, especially Twitter, to engage stakeholders, thank donors and build relationships with the media and parliamentarians.

Before we look at some ways in which charity CEOs can use social media successfully, I want to talk about why this group has a unique advantage. If you are a charity CEO, you have many things in your favour that leaders in business and politics would give their right arms to have.

Stories

I regularly talk to charity leaders whose organizations are doing great work around the world – everything from helping people following earthquakes, to supporting patients with good end-of-life care in hospices or campaigning for better rights for people with disabilities. There is a depth, richness and meaning to what they do which informs their passion – and it is a treasure trove of great content.

Every charity leader I've spoken to is leading an organization which is trying to change the world for the better, whether they are a tiny charity serving their local community or a huge global NGO. And they are working with amazing people, whether it is the beneficiaries they support or their dedicated colleagues.

If you are a charity leader, think about all the inspiring, moving or newsworthy stories you come across every day through your job. Then think about how you could tell them. The CEOs I've come across who do this really well will grab their phone and post something which tells this story on social media.

Inspiring stories are the reason why charity leaders get up and go to work every morning – and they are why people will follow them on social media. I've spoken to many charity leaders who bemoan the lack of budget or time to be a storyteller – but they may be ignoring the stories which are right in front of them. Think about anything that demonstrates how you are achieving your vision and mission, the exciting things you are working on every day, or how you've changed the lives of beneficiaries and their families.

You can't be a charity CEO without being a storyteller. It's in our sector's DNA. Whether you're writing a funding bid or talking to an MP or a beneficiary, you are surrounded by extraordinary stories, and you know their value. How else have you managed to get funding or broker support? Many of the stories you've heard could work brilliantly on social media, where they will help people remember you and your charity better.

Storytelling might sound like an indulgent, whimsical technique, but its purpose is deadly serious. It is an excellent way to show how your charity is having an impact. And that is critical to gaining public trust and confidence, which is vital for charities.

STORYTELLING TIPS:

- Think about the stories you hear every day, whether they're from service users, your fundraising team or staff. Your charity is changing lives. How can you share those stories in short social media posts?

- Storytelling is a skill. You need great images, strong characters and memorable details. There also needs to be narrative – although you don't have to tell the whole story in one post. How can you capture this?

- A picture is worth a thousand words. Taking good, clear pictures with your phone, or even short videos, will bring your social posts to life.

Cause

It's become a management cliché that every leader wants their organization to be part of a movement. Even a company like Coca Cola has a vision to 'make the world happier'.

But the only way to truly create a movement is to have a cause people want to get behind, and it's an awful lot harder to do this if you're CEO of a company selling stationery or soft drinks.

If you're a charity, you're genuinely doing something to help people or improve the world. This isn't bland Corporate Social Responsibility or a by-product of your work – it's the reason why you do what you do. As such, social media is a perfect way to find more people to support your work.

Before you post, think about the kind of reaction you want. How do you want people to feel? Outraged? Saddened? Reassured? What do you want people to do after that and how are you going to encourage them to do it? A powerful piece of content will make people stop and think.

If you tap into the right emotions, people are more likely to remember you, your charity and the cause you stand for – and could feel stirred into taking action.

HOW TO GET PEOPLE BEHIND YOUR CAUSE ON SOCIAL MEDIA:

- Make your cause relevant by sharing content that reinforces why your charity exists.

- Be bold. Social media is a very crowded space. You may need to be controversial, have strong opinions or be emotive – or you could be forgotten.

- Show why it matters. There are thousands of charities, all representing worthwhile causes. Tell people why they shouldn't think 'so what?'

Stakeholders

Charity CEOs are time poor and under huge pressure, juggling the pressures of leadership, media scrutiny and generating income. They won't have capacity to meet every beneficiary and all the stakeholders they would like to. As such, social media can be a very efficient way for them to talk to their stakeholders any time they want, from their smartphones.

In the past I had a senior role in a charity and I used social media to broker relationships with corporates, talk to beneficiaries and, on one occasion, score my CEO a meeting at Downing Street.

Charity CEOs have a natural aptitude for talking to a huge range of people. On a typical day they could be doing anything from a meeting at No 10 to visiting a community group or talking to service users. It's an incredibly varied job, and this needs to come across on social media as it shows transparency and demonstrates how leaders can make a difference.

Ideally your social media presence will be so strong that the people you really want to talk to will start following you, rather than you going to them.

Here are two interesting examples:

Deborah Alsina, CEO of Bowel Cancer UK, stands out by taking an empathetic and caring approach when talking to patients.
https://twitter.com/DeborahAlsina/status/1070792143554441216

Louie Macdonald, CEO of youth charity Young Scot, on the other hand, shows a real appreciation of volunteers and fundraisers. It's quick and easy but will be remembered.
https://twitter.com/Louisemac/status/1071393657146748928

TOP TIPS FOR MANAGING STAKEHOLDERS ON SOCIAL MEDIA:

- Map out all your key stakeholders, from MPs to funders, the media, partner organizations, beneficiaries, volunteers and fundraisers. Then start following the most influential ones.

- Plan how you can connect with them. This could be anything from commenting on a post they've shared. What do you want them to feel, think and then do?

- Use Twitter lists (you can set these to private) to track what particularly important groups, such as journalists, are saying.

Summary

Charity CEOs have a huge advantage when it comes to social media, which puts them ahead of leaders from the public and private sectors. Here are four key points to bear in mind:

- There's a group of charity CEOs who are using social media as part of their jobs already. If your board thinks you are wasting your time on Twitter, show them the previous winners from the Social CEOs awards,[2] which recognizes charity leaders active on social media.

- Your charity will have stories that would work well on social media. Where could you find them and how can you use them to engage people?

- Movements and campaigns can take off quickly on social media. What could you post that would mobilize people behind your charity's cause?

- Social media is a very efficient and constructive way to manage stakeholders. Do you know who they all are? What content would you use to engage them?

10

Living in glass houses: How the social CEO manages risk

Martin Thomas

Thanks to the digital revolution, chief executives now live in glass houses. An ill-judged remark can be broadcast to the world in an instant.

—THE ECONOMIST

This is how *The Economist* summed up how many CEOs view the use of social media as a business and leadership tool.[1] It is all too easy for social media evangelists to dismiss these concerns as irrelevant or irrational, but in many C-Suite environments social media is perceived as a risky activity. This sentiment is fed by high-profile incidents such as the $40 million fine imposed by the Securities and Exchange Commission (SEC) on Elon Musk and Tesla for issuing a tweet that contained what the regulators considered to be inaccurate information about the company's financial plans.

The risk of directors disclosing inappropriate or misleading information in financially regulated companies is particularly acute. As Elon Musk discovered, there are strict rules imposed by the regulatory bodies about the disclosure of price-sensitive information. Even the most innocent post or tweet by a senior manager, such as alluding to a forthcoming investment announcement, can technically be in breach of the rules. The regulators are comfortable with social media being used as a channel for corporate and investor information, but insist that potentially share-sensitive information should not be shared with an individual's followers (no matter how large their following) before it is shared with the general public through official corporate channels.

Perceived levels of risk vary by business category. Some business sectors are simply more regulated or controversial than others, which is why you tend to find clusters of C-Suite social media activity in certain industries, such as technology and consumer goods, but relatively low levels of activity in pharmaceuticals, alcohol, finance and gambling. The CEO of a UK-based bookmaker quit Twitter within days of setting up an account after finding himself in a continuous online argument with opponents of fixed-odds betting terminals. If their Twitter stream is simply going to become a magnet for vociferous critics, largely uninterested in having a reasoned and civil debate, you can understand why many leaders in high-profile and occasionally controversial sectors choose to steer well clear.

Organizations can exacerbate the risks by putting senior managers into 'no win' situations. A UK-based utility company created a reputational 'road-crash' when it decided to schedule a Twitter-based question and answer session, featuring its customer-service director, on the day it announced it was increasing customer prices by 10 per cent. The unfortunate director was forced to deal with a maelstrom of largely negative and occasional hostile comments and loaded questions, such as 'Would it be OK to burn the corpses of your board of directors when I can no longer afford heating?', which I doubt was covered by his question and answer brief. By providing a platform for public protest, the company was simply exacerbating an already difficult situation. This is not how to create a meaningful and constructive dialogue between senior managers and their customers.

Crisis situations will inevitably place the C-Suite's use of social media under intense scrutiny. Media and other stakeholders, seeking information or reassurance during a crisis, are increasingly likely to expect to make direct contact with the senior leadership team through their personal social channels. This may further discourage C-Suite participation in social media – why put yourself in the front line when you have the option of hiding behind official corporate channels? That said, there is an equally strong counter-argument that CEOs should personalize crisis situations by using their social channels to communicate directly with stakeholders. This personal involvement can help to humanize the company's response and send a clear message to staff and external audiences that the senior team is in command of the situation. However, a crisis is not the time to discover that you do not have policies on critical issues, cannot access critical facts or the people to deal with them and do not have the skills, resources or support system to manage a high volume of comments and questions.

The risks associated with the use of social media in a C-Suite 'glass house', in which senior leaders are subject to internal compliance and external scrutiny, are real and potentially significant: corporate and individual reputations can be harmed, career prospects damaged and financial penalties occasionally imposed. However, the vast majority of risks can be avoided or minimized by adhering to five simple principles:

1 Understand and observe the regulations. As demonstrated by Elon Musk's unfortunate run-in with the authorities, leaders operating in regulated sectors face constraints on their use of social media, and those working for publicly listed companies must be wary of disclosing information on social media that may be price sensitive.

   To counter these risks, it can be helpful for executive teams to agree subject areas about which they will never comment, such as investment decisions, potential partnerships (even praising the performance of a potential partner could be a risk) and planned changes to company structures and manpower. Corporate compliance specialists can play an important role in educating the C-Suite about the appropriate use of social media and putting in place the necessary controls to spot and deal with (the hopefully rare) mistakes.

2 Stick to lower risk topics. This is about being smart, rather than being bland; for example, Apple's Tim Cook uses his Twitter feed to attack discrimination and support gay rights, while Richard Branson uses his channels to campaign for the end of the death penalty.

   Leaders are expected to take a position, especially on issues that impact directly on the performance of their business or the welfare of their employees, but they need to be wary of expressing potentially divisive opinions, especially where these are not shared by the rest of the senior team. Expressing overt political opinions in an increasingly polarized political climate is likely to be especially problematic, as a few CEOs have discovered when declaring their views on Donald Trump or Brexit.

Sharing lifestyle, as opposed to professional, content is likely to be far less risky and adds another dimension to a leader's online persona. We like to see the real person behind the corporate mask – for example Tim Cook's tweet, 'Inspiring day hiking @YosemiteNPS. Hats off to the Park Service', which generated almost 6,000 likes and showed his 2.6 million followers a different, less 'techie' side to his personality. Where professionals need to be cautious is where this lifestyle content blends into home and family life. Mark Zuckerberg is happy to show images of him playing with his children – he no doubt sees this as a way of humanizing his reputation – but other senior executives are understandably less keen on exposing their families to the glare of publicity and the risk of inappropriate comments.

3 Put in place a support system. The most effective users of social media in the boardroom are smart enough to put a support system in place to deal with the volume of comments and posts. They recognize that they cannot manage their social media activities from the back of a taxi or running between meetings, but need the support of their PAs and

their social media teams. This may offend the social media purists, who will claim that relying on other people to occasionally tweet on your behalf is inauthentic, but all of the global leaders who are acknowledged as expert social media communicators, including Barak Obama and Richard Branson, rely to some extent on a support system, especially when it comes to responding to the sheer volume of social media messages they receive. I know when Richard Branson replies to one of my tweeted questions that it is probably not his fingers on the reply button, but at least I receive a response. Even Mark Zuckerberg employs teams of people to script his posts and films, handle his interactions with followers and protect his online brand.

4　Start with lower risk channels and approaches. LinkedIn, in particular, is a 'gateway drug' for the social CEO. It is less time consuming – you only need to post content or comments three or four times a week and check in for five minutes a day to generate value from the channel – and far less adversarial. The risks compared with maintaining a Twitter channel are far smaller. If you do decide to use Twitter or Instagram, start by being an observer, rather than a commentator. Not only will you pick up invaluable insights into the opinions of customers, opinion formers and other stakeholders but you will also gain a better understanding of the tone and style to adopt when you decide to start engaging proactively with these audiences.

5　Don't be too adversarial. You may think it makes you look tough, and there are a few high-profile, social-media-using

CEOs who like to share controversial opinions in the manner of online 'shock-jocks', but it is invariably counter-productive. Have fun, try not to get into extended arguments – especially late at night when we can all, on occasion, get somewhat disinhibited – and don't say anything that you would not want your mother to read.

PART THREE

SOCIAL CEOs IN THEIR OWN WORDS

11

The sports sector

Brett Gosper

All business sectors are facing the challenges of competing in a context of high-velocity technological change. That change is disrupting both access to and the attention of consumers, whose loyalty we seek to acquire. Added to this is the need in such a rapidly evolving landscape to make quality decisions at high speed.

In sport, as in all industries, it is no longer what you know but how fast you learn. Engaging and interacting on social media is critical to learning about and understanding your target audience in real time.

In the case of World Rugby, rugby union's governing body, there are two specific challenges:

Firstly, we are not dealing with the 'usual' consumer. This is not a person walking the aisles of a supermarket or browsing online, where choices between brands can often boil down to a question of familiarity or apathy. The core consumer of rugby – as with any sport – is truly emotional. They are opinionated, passionate and fiercely loyal to the point of being possessive. They can also be tribal in their obsessive love of a team or the sport itself. They are more than consumers – they are fans. It is this high-octane, emotional connection between fan and sport that requires understanding, empathy and careful management.

Secondly, the world of sports federations has a complex stakeholder dimension that adds the political to the managerial. An international federation is an elected board that is representative of each country's aspirations that make up its membership. Added to this is an appointed CEO and management team that partner with the elected membership to ensure strategic and executional momentum.

Conventional business sectors operate with a professional management team that answers to shareholders and are bottom line- and market share-driven. This difference does not necessarily make sports federations less effective, but it does bring a dimension of political complexity that can challenge unity and clarity of purpose if not well managed by the unique partnership.

Given these two specific differences, it is clear to me that social media can not only work to counter some of the potential challenges in these areas, but also be a potent tool to leverage these specific areas of stakeholder difference.

As opposed to the consumer, the fan demands involvement in the leadership of their sport. They want to know who is taking care of it, how we are making it safer and healthier, how we are enhancing their experience at home and in stadia, what we are doing to ensure the sport grows around the world, how we simplify and improve laws and how we eradicate foul play and doping – among many other concerns.

These are the preoccupations of a fan as opposed to the more indifferent demands of a consumer. In this context, social media interaction provides a unique opportunity to talk directly with fans in a way that is unfiltered and unhindered by traditional media and marketing channels. More importantly, it is a two-way communication where 'receiving' is every bit as important as transmitting. Used in the right way, social media can be the ultimate real-time focus group – often personally brutal but always a source of high-speed enlightenment.

One of the hardest questions for any business to answer is what they wish to stand for in the minds of their audience. When you are a sports federation with multiple stakeholders and members – often with their own national agendas – a focused, single-minded answer to that question is not easy to establish and communicate.

Once again, social media can not only provide the platform to project a clear voice to the world but also offer a galvanizing direction and clarity to diverse internal stakeholders, guiding them and reminding them of their own mission and role in furthering the federation's purpose.

At World Rugby we are obsessed with growing our global fan base and participation. In recent years this has meant moving the needle more clearly from the emphasis on regulation to that of inspiration. The changing of our brand from the obscure (for those not inside the sport) International Rugby Board (IRB) to the outward facing 'World Rugby' clearly provided us with the opportunity to position the federation as the global voice of 'brand rugby'.

This is a statement of leadership that relies heavily on the intelligent and creative use of social media if we are to successfully transition our brand towards the 'platinum' status of being a global movement. An annual global survey by Red Torch in 2017 placed World Rugby number one out of thirty-five Olympic-recognized international sports federations in social media usage. This is testament to our efforts to prioritize this area.

The CEO stepping up

Social media is now critical to all businesses, and few would question its power in shaping market perceptions. More controversial is the personal use of social media by CEOs.

When I arrived at the then International Rugby Board in 2012, I was struck by how aloof the IRB was as an organization. We were not listed in the phone directory until the mid-1990s, there was no name or branding outside our building in Dublin and there were few displays of corporate personality and public empathy. Our communication was efficient and authoritative, as was the habit of many governing bodies, and there did seem to be a view that the media and public were to be engaged only in a formal way. At the time I felt that this formality was often interpreted with suspicion by the media and public.

While I was aware of the risks and dangers of using social media, I was convinced that my personal use of it would be a clear and dramatic way to help shift perceptions from us as a guarded and even secretive organization to a more open and engaging one. My theory being that a listening organization that was better understood and more human was one that could significantly create more positive momentum.

Any communication vacuum is filled with interpretation, almost always in a negative way. Personal use of social media provided me with the means to attempt to drive a media and public reappraisal of the then IRB while also listening to opinion and perceptions.

I did this by immediately following and connecting with every influential rugby and sports journalist and influencer on Twitter. They would follow me back. It meant I was accessible to all and able to fill some of that vacuum and personalize the leadership of the organization. This one-to-one connection seemed to create more empathy with the media, who were able to question and discuss World Rugby's personalized views in full view of the public or via Direct Messaging if they wished.

While it never guaranteed agreement, I feel it created some respect for what we were trying to do. While the novelty of a CEO on Twitter has long passed, I do think empathy and respect for that non-stop direct connection continue. The proximity enabled better explanations and understanding for media and fans. This was around complex and controversial issues such as concussion scrum engagement protocols, injury rates, law changes, referee/disciplinary decisions (always the most emotive) as well as clarifying our views and ambitions around the Rugby World Cup, the Olympics, Sevens and club rugby. Some of these areas required real-time engagement to ensure full understanding by media and fans – something a press release can't always satisfy.

I have definitely made mistakes along the way and have learned from those mistakes. In the beginning I sometimes gave a view or an opinion on Twitter that, due to my focus on fans and the media, flew in the face of the usual World Rugby communication channels. It was usually in the area of player discipline, and it created a lot of negative reaction from our member unions; I was even ticked off several times by the Executive Committee for influencing or circumventing the judiciary. There was a move to ban my use of Twitter but I was able to argue the overwhelming benefits for the organization, and common sense prevailed.

While a good bit of public controversy is always healthy for boosting your Twitter following, a negative public storm can be unnecessarily stressful to many, and I have learned from this.

Examples include asking that a player be punished to the full extent of the law for defying rugby's hard-earned values by spitting on another international player. This was a tweet during the game and well before it went to a judicial hearing, which could have prejudiced the hearing. On another occasion, I tweeted that we would appeal an over-lenient sanction (by our own judiciary) for a foot to head incident in an international game.

These tweets created great friction with the federations involved, as I had not managed internal communications before going public. This is an easy mistake to make on Twitter as one is reacting to public outrage, and the temptation to move fast is immense.

Even with careful thought and following a career in advertising, where I was in the business of understanding consumer reactions, I couldn't always accurately predict a public reaction. I once created public outrage in Wales by commenting when England's cricket team did not get out of the pool phase at Cricket World Cup. It is always good news for the success of an international tournament that the host progresses well in their own tournament. I tweeted that 'it wasn't something we want to see in England 2015'. The Welsh fans interpreted this as a potential bias from World Rugby, as they were in the same pool as England and some implied we might work to influence the match officials in that way. This was ludicrous in my mind at the time, but the perception is always more understandable with hindsight.

Since those early days, experience has helped me to avoid unnecessary controversy, but I am always aware that one tweet can spark a forest fire of controversy.

Now it is not just the CEO of World Rugby who tweets, but also the Chairman Bill Beaumont and Vice-Chairman Agustin Pichot, who manages a lively Twitter account with a significant following. Several of our executive committees and a large number of our staff are also now very active on Twitter and Instagram. All this adds up to a weight of positive, authentic information flow for World Rugby and the sport of rugby in general. It also increases the risk of communication mishaps, so we ensure we train our staff in social media usage as we do also for referees and players who venture into the space.

Twitter has become the natural habitat of the 'stars', including musicians, television personalities, artists, actors and sports celebrities. These people also tend to be dealing with a passionate fan base rather than just a consumer audience. In more recent times politicians have taken to Twitter. Again, this sits well with the medium, as people want to get to know the personality of their politicians and the politicians themselves are attempting to build a larger following or movement.

One might argue therefore that social media is no place for a serious corporate-minded CEO.

The difference is that CEOs should not use social media to promote themselves, but to further the connection between their organization and their audience. If that audience is fan-based, that's perfect. If you are trying to turn your brand into a movement, even better. If that audience is made up of passionate consumers, then that will also work.

If you are the CEO of a low-interest consumer sector, then usage is not out of the question, but returns on time investment are likely to be modest. It depends on message shaping. Even the CEO of a tyre company can become an evangelist for the environment or work conditions. The public will ultimately decide if you are interesting to 'listen' to – and gathering enough of them will help shape the perceptions of your company or brand.

Here are my five tips for other CEOs in the sports sector.

1   Be yourself. Followers know when a social media account is managed by the PR department or someone else. Followers aren't just seeking information – they are seeking understanding. Twitter is a personal medium, so an absence of personality means followers will turn off.

2   Your view is the organization's view. It is impossible to say that 'this is just my view' or 'all views my own'. As a CEO your view on social media will be seen as the organization's view, so be very aware (and be sure) that you are conveying the view of an entire organization.

3   Don't react too fast. The provocative tweets fired at you are designed to get a reaction. It is tempting to react quickly in order to land a winning counter punch or embarrass the aggressor. The most aggressive tweets usually come from those with the fewest followers. If you reply you are giving that person your readership, a coverage they do not deserve.

If it is important to react, then take the time to calm down or show a reactive draft tweet to your PR head or an advisor. If you are tired, jetlagged or have been drinking, never tweet.

4   Get your facts right. As a CEO you will not be forgiven for sloppiness if you get your numbers, spellings, names and dates wrong – and it will reflect on your organization. Media loves to pick up on these errors and amplify them to the public.

5   Demand content. While a CEO often believes that his or her words are enthralling, sharing interesting visuals, infographics, videos or other compelling content will be far more interesting for your followers. Put pressure on your organization to provide these for you. And don't just send out the corporate content as is – give more meaning and context to it from a leadership perspective.

The final point I would make is that, if you are going to spend the extra hours managing a personal/public social media account (I spend at least one hour a day on Twitter, and often two), you have to enjoy doing it. You need to enjoy crafting words and jousting with followers and be genuinely interested in people's views and passionate about providing answers and guidance.

Getting started is the hard part. I suggest that you begin your social media life as a follower, watching and learning how other role models use it. Then, when you feel ready ... 'hello world'.

12

The healthcare sector

Julia Hanigsberg

I was a late adopter of social media. I remember asking a young lawyer on one of my teams more than a decade ago, 'What is Facebook anyway?' Her response was this: 'Everyone who works for you who is young is on it!' I also remember asking another professional on a different team (with some derision) why would I want to get news in 140-character bites when I get a daily newspaper at my door (he didn't have a great answer!).

Today, with a monthly blog, Instagram and Facebook accounts and tens of thousands of tweets later, I guess I'm a convert. Social media has become an important part of my identity as a healthcare CEO. So, how did I go from a sceptic to writing a chapter on being a social CEO for this book?

One part of the answer is that I've been lucky to have great social media mentors. When I worked in a large university, I had students as my 'reverse mentors' who coached me. And *through* Twitter, a terrific social media expert named Lina Duque reached out to me and has been a coach and mentor (and friend!) ever since.

My work

In order to tell the story of being a social CEO, it makes sense to talk a bit about the challenges I face on a day-to-day basis *outside* of the social realm.

I am president and CEO of Holland Bloorview Kids Rehabilitation Hospital. Established in 1899, Holland Bloorview is located in Toronto, Canada, and serves children and youth from across Ontario and Canada from infancy to young adulthood. The hospital sees clients with over 2,000 unique diagnoses annually. Our work is to support children and youth living with disability, medical complexity, illness and injury. A holistic approach is taken to assist young people in achieving their goals. This includes physical and cognitive development as well as life skills such as employment readiness, transitioning to adult healthcare and social services and friendship. Children and youth also have access to programming in music, arts, fitness, science and technology. Holland Bloorview is also an academic health sciences centre, which means that it trains the next generation of clinical professionals: doctors, nurses, therapists of all kinds and many others. In addition, it is in the top forty Canadian research hospitals, where researchers are working on the solutions to change the future for children and youth.

My number one priority is high-quality, safe, compassionate and coordinated health care that is centred around children, youth and their families. My team is extraordinary and makes miracles every day, but I know that the healthcare experience for families is far from perfect.

For example, I hear frequently from families how fragmented the healthcare system is. Why, as one mother asked me, is she expected to be the general contractor of her child's care, keeping track of medications, specialist appointments, transitions between hospitals and home, back to family physician and in the school as well? My challenge is to work with other leaders across healthcare, social services and government (and more) to bring order to that fragmentation. And by the way, that mother I referenced is someone I follow and interact with on Instagram and Twitter.

A high proportion of our clients are children with disabilities who need not only tremendous medical care (and research to advance that care) but also acceptance and inclusion to achieve their most meaningful futures. Instead they face stigma and barriers. As one of our young clients tells us, she frequently lunches alone in the cafeteria at high school and her peers don't see past her wheelchair to the person she really is: a creative ambitious young woman who plans to be a successful novelist and a mother and won't let her cerebral palsy get in the way. That same young woman and I follow each other on Instagram.

Another inevitable challenge is the cost of providing care. We are fortunate in Canada to have publicly funded healthcare, but those funds are scarce and the costs of providing care are constantly increasing. We have to be great stewards of the financial resources we have and creatively stretch every dollar.

The relentless march of technology is another inevitability and a cost-driver. And while technology is a boon and necessity, it is also a burden. Type 'doctors and technology' into Google and you'll be flooded with search results that lament how much clinicians hate electronic health records (which were supposed to save time and money) and essays predicting a future where artificial intelligence will replace much of the healthcare workforce (a contention with which I disagree).

Finally, our people are our single greatest resource. Burnout among clinicians is a serious reality, so I am laser-focused on how to promote team wellness. We also need to plan and recruit for the *future* of healthcare while being mired in the challenges of the present. To use a uniquely Canadian metaphor, we need to, in the words of hockey great Wayne Gretsky, 'skate to where the puck is going, not where it has been'.

Social leadership

So how does any of this relate to social media? Well, social media is an important part of healthcare leadership because of the need to stay on top of these challenges within the context of the pace of change and the challenges of complexity.

The pace of change means that it is a struggle to keep on top of what you need to know to be an effective healthcare leader. I use Twitter as a tool to be engaged in some of the most current thinking and in dialogue with some of those thought leaders. I use social media as a rapid and omnipresent content delivery system that helps me identify and consume information, including health science research and leadership/strategy advice.

The complexity means that sources of information and knowledge from different sectors and thinkers are important in helping me approach the range of problems I'm thinking about. The breadth and variety of thinkers I'm exposed to on social media gives me insights that I can share with my team.

Through social media I not only read about but get to *interact* with academics, researchers and thought leaders from around the corner and around the globe. Perhaps even more importantly, I'm exposed to thinking from patients, caregivers, advocates and critics who are unlikely to be published in traditional sources. The challenge of being in dialogue with non-privileged viewpoints, whether or not I agree with them, is incredibly valuable for my ongoing thinking and personal development as a leader.

My unique approach to social media

My approach has been to use social media to be an extension of transparency in my leadership and to be the digital equivalent of the world's best cocktail party!

If you imagine the quintessential open-door leadership approach, how much more effective is it if that door is open to all of Twitter? I've had young professionals reach out to me over Twitter to ask for career advice. I've had parents of children waiting for admission to our hospital connect with me by DM (direct message – a private way of communicating on Twitter) to ask questions, giving me the ability to connect them to the right people on my team, or to easy-to-access online resources. Members of my own team share their research or experience, and I get to amplify the impact they are making by sharing with my network. I connect with scientists thousands of kilometres and multiple time zones from where I live to hear about the most interesting and provocative new thinking.

I was new to healthcare four years ago, and social media accelerated my networking with leaders in the field. Before day one at Holland Bloorview, people who I was going to be working with were following me on Twitter so I hit the ground running with those on my new team who felt like they knew me and who I could rely on to help extend in-person relationships.

My Twitter feed is a window into who I am and what I care about. That is in the context of the professional me (healthcare/public sector leader), the engaged me (advocate for women in leadership, girls in STEM and disability stigma-busting) and the personal me (mom, wife, dog owner, reader).

That combination of the personal and professional is, for me, the essence of success on social media. To be effective, your social media presence needs to reflect your whole self and needs to be authentic and interactive. One of the best things is how people I meet in real life for the first time will feel like they already know and trust me because of prior engagement over social media. This could be because of a scientific breakthrough I tweeted about, but just as often it is because I shared a photo of Golda (my dog), a recipe or a novel recommendation.

Challenges

As much as my social media presence is personal to me, at the same time, as a CEO, whatever I do or say publicly reflects upon my organization. I treat my social media as an extension of myself and have to use judgement so that I don't inadvertently put the hospital's reputation at risk – I think I do a pretty good job at that balance.

I remember once being told by a communications professional that something I put in my blog about what I was currently reading wasn't 'relatable'. But it was literally what I was currently reading! Relatable or not, it stayed in because ... authenticity!

However, there have been cases where someone has reacted negatively to something I've posted. For example, I touched a nerve when I expressed sympathy for the family of an accused perpetrator of a deadly and devastating crime. The context was the heartbroken mother of the accused lamenting failed multiple attempts to access mental health resources for her adult child. Fortunately, I was able to reach out over social media to an individual who had been particularly hurt by my comments and diffuse the situation, but I've seen those emotion-laden moments explode over social. The public nature of social media always includes some risk.

Five social media tips for CEOs in the healthcare sector

If you are thinking of embracing social media as a healthcare leader (and I think you should), here are five tips to consider:

1   Give it a try and be prepared to learn as you go.

    I started out by following and 'listening' for a while before I got up the nerve to post. Find respected people or people you personally admire who are active on whatever social channel you want to try and learn from what they do, including things like frequency, style, use of hashtags, emojis and other social tactics. On Twitter, look for the feeds of some of the people you admire most as leaders or commentators. Then develop your personal style.

2   Neither be intimidated by nor be focused on numbers of followers, likes and so on.

Social media companies rely on our obsession with these very things and the dopamine rush of the 'like' to fuel our obsession with (and some say addiction to) social media. Resist! Be real. Share and consume what you find meaningful (and fun). Interact with people who fascinate and challenge you. Be a thoughtful, literate and critical consumer of information. Be impact-focused rather than followers-focused.

3   Don't think you are too busy for social.

Of course you are busy. The beauty of social is it will take exactly the amount of time you want to give it and not a minute less or a minute more. If you don't trust yourself not to get pulled down a digital rabbit hole, set a timer on your phone. You can be a social CEO in just fifteen minutes a day.

4   Share what other people are posting.

Be an amplifier and help other voices get heard, particularly people with less power or privilege than you might have. Give marginalized voices a place at the centre.

5   Use social media to connect with your own team and
    prospective employees.

    Even if yours is a small organization and you are a master
    at 'management by wandering around', it is unlikely as CEO
    that you will be able to connect with every member of your
    team as often as you wish (I know I can't). Social can be how
    you can connect with everyone – especially people who work
    different hours or other places than you do as CEO. Social
    media will never replace personally getting to the satellite
    location or connecting in person with staff who work the
    night shift, but it is a superb way to be broadly available.

Concluding thoughts

I never thought of myself as a social CEO. Our identities are composed
of many elements, and social media can be a vehicle to exploring those
different parts of ourselves with multiple communities. My leadership
identity – who am I as a CEO in healthcare – is one of those multiple
identities. Social media has been there to help me become the leader
I am today and I'm grateful for the global community it helps me to
be a part of. If that is being a social CEO, then I guess I am one – and
all the better for it.

13

The manufacturing sector

Chris Mason

'You should be on Twitter' – five words which were immediately obvious to me. It was July 2009 and I was midway through my fourteen-year career with the Society of Motor Manufacturers and Traders in the UK. I was keen to learn more about how new media could support me as I embarked upon leading a new subsidiary we had recently created.

Those words turned out to be good advice, even though it was quite a step into the unknown for me at the time. While social media was already embedded in the fabric of society, it wasn't the all-consuming form of media it is today.

For me, Twitter in particular soon became a fundamental part of my life and continues to be the place I go first thing every day to catch up. It's also something I revisit throughout the day to keep up to speed with international news, industry developments, colleagues and professional friends' activities – and, of course, to deliver important messages of my own.

Best of all, over the last decade, Twitter has enabled me to feel constantly connected with 'my world' and has played an important role as I've developed my international network and profile. The 'real time' information flow I have created through the people and organizations I follow, which provides others with a reciprocal access into my world, is positive in so many ways.

As I consider the upside of my engagement with Twitter, what is clear is that I have benefited immeasurably by being immersed in a daily newsfeed from the automotive and mobility systems engineering community. This keeps me up to speed on the latest developments as they happen, wherever the news comes from. This is a truly great international window to have access to.

Of course, this form of information flow has its positives and negatives. It clearly benefits me to be knowledgeable and up to speed, sustaining the important international perspective I like to maintain across our industry. But it can also mean my influence is tailored to my preference, which in turn can create a blinkered vision, especially when applied to news and politics. So it's also important for me to use Twitter as one part of a mix of news, information and opinion to ensure I'm scanning a broad landscape and not restricting my knowledge-harvesting ability.

As I think back to those early days of my Twitter engagement, it's interesting to consider that I didn't plan a business case or conduct a business need evaluation. I just got involved, not knowing at the time that ten years down the line I would firmly believe that social media is best exploited from a leadership perspective in this way.

I still have no metric or performance measurement applied to my use of Twitter, it wouldn't feel right to me – the same reason why I retain sole operational use of my account. It's so easy to tell when an individual's account is being 'managed' for them, trotting out dull corporate messaging as part of the communications outreach machine, delivered by a ghostwriter. It just doesn't work.

This form of media has an organic truth about it which can't be delivered for you, in much the same way it's not something that can be written into a business plan. If you have a stated objective to deliver a certain number of tweets per day, hit high-volume follower targets, or allow a team member to manage your account, then you've got the wrong strategy in my view.

If I'm clear on what the wrong strategy is, then what's the right strategy? I think it's simple: if you are of interest to the community around you, you're in the game.

On this basis, it's a pretty brutal place to be, as the 'market' really does decide, nothing else. Get it right and you'll achieve sustained and consistent engagement, get it wrong and there's simply no one listening, which is a pretty lonely virtual place to be, right?

I was going to add that you just can't buy an online social presence, but I guess you can. It just won't be truly your online presence and is therefore hollow in my view. Much more rewarding and beneficial is to get it right yourself and sustain your community's interest in you, learning how to engage and what to share – and being open to showing the world something of your personality.

You will then have the correct ingredients to successfully utilize social media as part of your mix of messaging outreach. You will build your following and assert your influence. Just be careful how much influence you try to assert, as the 'unfollow' button is merely a click away!

To summarize this part of my chapter, I guess you could say that sustaining the community one develops is key. But merely not *losing* them is not the goal. Instead, utilizing the additional outreach opportunity social media has created to deliver a valuable contribution to the community around you should be your goal. If you're able to deliver this as a leader, you extend your influence and increase your organization's profile.

I would therefore propose that any leader's personal engagement with social media is a relevant and tangible leadership currency.

A new leadership style

Back in 2009 no one knew that social media had the potential to inform and indeed form a new leadership style, enabling leaders to operate in a visible, accessible, open and engaging manner, using social channels to reach their target audience(s) directly and immediately.

Just like all leaders, my leadership styles are defined through emotional intelligence (EI). I'm fortunate to have a natural collaborative and participative style, which lends itself to engaging and influencing people through being a part of the community. These character traits are great ingredients to be able to bring to the mix when leading an international membership organization as I do.

These traits are also what make social media an obvious addition to my professional toolkit – it's basically intuitive and a very natural extension to what I do. Perhaps not everyone sees the same picture, as their EI may make them a different kind of leader, one that's as natural to them as my leadership style is to me.

While we didn't realize it at the time, social media has enabled leaders to become more engaged and, through doing so, increasingly closer to the pulse of their community. The amount of times I meet new people and, during the initial conversation, they make reference to something that could only have been learned through online engagement is significant.

'I see you're just back from China,' 'We were at the same industry event in Detroit' and 'Congratulations on launching the Foundation in India' are all recent comments I've received from industry colleagues during an opening discussion that I know derived from my use of Twitter. They have been excellent 'ice-breakers', as there's a common reference point and also a mutual understanding that we're already connected, even before we actually meet.

What's also important in my view is how we can use social media to open the door a little into our personal lives. In my experience, reference to relevant downtime interests and hobbies often helps, as it ensures an initial familiarity and often confirms common interests, encouraging a positive perception of an individual away from their professional role.

I'm certain I've gained much over the years through being engaged on social media, offering my thoughts and opinions and opening the door to some of my day-to-day life and welcoming others to join me.

I can hear the words of one or two previous bosses ringing in my ears at this point: 'Why the hell would you want that?' My response is simple and consistent: 'Why the hell wouldn't I?'

The fact that my strategy has been sustained for a decade, unchanged, and has become an increasingly intuitive and effective part of my life tells you all you need to know.

Before I finish this chapter, consider this final thought process.

The mobility evolution

The industry in which I have worked for over thirty years is a rapidly changing technological world, creating the safe, sustainable and affordable transport solutions of the future. The traditional automobile manufacturing industry is changing fast as it transitions into the mobility services sector of tomorrow. This means that the leaders of some of the world's largest and most recognized brands are shaping the autonomous, connected, shared and increasingly electric future of transportation.

Vehicles will be connected with each other and with the infrastructure around them, as they become incredibly advanced mobility devices, with artificial intelligence and deep learning set to deliver the smart and clean mobility services which will address the societal challenges created over the previous hundred years of ever-increasing consumer and business demand for the automobile.

This change will also bring a different business model and different consumer behaviour to our industry. We're already seeing the 'big brands' redefining and restructuring their businesses as they prepare to morph from volume manufacturers to service providers. As they do, the value chain changes and new ecosystems emerge, signalling a new and vastly different set of relationships where engagement with consumers will be increasingly direct. This means we will all expect to be connected as a matter of course.

To contribute effectively to this world and operate in a way that the community around us will increasingly demand, leaders will need to be visible, contributing and proactively engaged with their community. I'm not even sure this will be defined as social, or media – I think it will just be what evolves from what has been created over the last decade.

Meanwhile, would I consider myself a social CEO? Absolutely.

14

The charity sector

David Barker

Charities in the UK are currently under the most intense public, regulatory and media scrutiny than they have ever been. Never before has such a penetrating spotlight been shone on how charities are going about their daily business. A number of 'scandals', the unearthing of some poor fundraising practices and several media exposes have all fuelled a public and political hunger for greater transparency, regulation and increased scrutiny.

According to a number of opinion polls, trust and public confidence in the UK's third sector hit an all-time low in 2018 (although we should not forget that it still remains higher than many other sectors).

This recent spotlight is both reassuring and worrying. Reassuring to know that any bad practices, poor management or damaging decisions are being highlighted and rooted out, but equally worrying to see that the misplaced actions or decisions of a few are tarnishing the image of the many. Enter the CEO.

Clearly any successful organization or business requires strong leadership to develop, grow and survive. In the UK there are over

167,000 charities all trying to do their best for the people they serve. Although the title of this book is *The Social CEO* we mustn't forget that a significant majority of charities in the UK don't have a CEO – but they will have leaders or senior volunteers leading the charge. In this chapter therefore, the term 'social CEO' refers to any senior 'leader' (paid or voluntary) within the charity sector.

So, what is on the mind of every charity leader? As a charity CEO – and also a consultant working with CEOs and charities/nonprofits of all sizes – I have my own views. But as part of the research for this chapter I spoke with many CEOs about their daily challenges and why they have chosen (or in some cases refused) to embrace social media as part of their leadership role.

All charities rely on money to do their work, so it's hardly surprising that the challenge of raising income sits high on the CEOs' list of worries. 'You can't change the world without balancing the books', says John May, Secretary General of the Duke of Edinburgh's International Award. This is a sentiment held by many CEOs. Charities have created a perfectly formed virtuous circle of 'the more money you raise, the better you can do to help your beneficiaries, so the more successful you become and the more money you need to raise', explained May.

According to Caron Bradshaw, CEO of Charity Finance Group, 'We're in a perfect storm – massive need and squeezed resources', a view also held by Matt Hyde, CEO of the Scouts. 'Maximising our impact and coping with increasing demand from beneficiaries at a time when there are often diminishing resources and increased regulation are typical challenges faced by all charities', he says.

Whatever the priority, one thing is clear. Strong, open and visible leadership is one of the key, critical lines on any CEO's job description.

Never before has there been a greater need for charity CEOs to lead from the front, be visible and use every opportunity to inform, educate, inspire (and reassure) their supporters and beneficiaries about their work. Strong 'social leadership' in a growing 'social age' has a key part to play. Over the next few pages we will hear from a variety of charity leaders about how they have made the transition into a social CEO.

Early beginnings

My first foray into social media (for work reasons) was probably more about satisfying a slightly voyeuristic need to finding out what others were up to rather than having any fancy strategic reasoning or understanding about how it could help me to be a better leader. In fact, I was a cynic who needed some convincing as to why anyone really cared whether you had 'just eaten breakfast' or were 'on a bus', as some of the early tweets I viewed declared.

I also wrestled a lot with how I could justify spending precious time on social media. I had no idea or understanding of the benefits it might bring to me in my role as a senior leader in the charity sector – and I certainly had no comprehension of where the journey might take me.

However, as a fervent believer in the old adage that 'if you don't try, you'll never know' I decided to set up a Twitter account. On 24 February 2009, I took the plunge with a simple statement of fact: 'Signing up to Twitter', I proudly declared to the world with my first tweet. It was followed swiftly by another inspired declaration: 'Watching tweets', I told the Twitter masses as I began to avidly follow people who I thought might be interesting and relevant. And so it all began.

Bringing some order to my thinking

Having thrown myself in, I decided to spend time in four key areas:

Listening

Using Twitter to listen and monitor can be a revelation – by setting up lists (which helped me sort the 'tweet' from the chaff) – I was able to see and hear first-hand what people were saying about the issues that matter to the charity and the people we serve. Social media is a real-time temperature check which is helpful, enlightening, inspiring, occasionally painful but most of all tremendously insightful. James Blake, CEO at the Youth Hostel Association, agrees: 'It's a really good way of quickly understanding what is going on; feeling the mood music; ensuring we can react quickly to events.'

Researching

It is quite stunning (and a bit scary) just how much you can find out about people, issues and organizations through social media. Whether it's a quick piece of 'social research' in advance of meeting someone or trying to reach out and connect with relevant and useful individuals/ opinion formers as part of a networking and influencing programme, they are all tremendously valuable uses of social media (particularly

so with LinkedIn and Twitter). I am constantly surprised how helpful
this research and insight can be.

Broadcasting

Amplifying your organizational messaging, being an ambassador for
the cause, connecting with stakeholders and being an extension of
your organizational brand are all important parts of a CEO's social
media broadcasting.

Matthew Hodson, Social CEOs Award[1] winner in 2017 and CEO
of NAM, strongly advocates for the time he spends broadcasting on
social media: 'I consider the time I spend on social media to be a good
investment. Twitter has allowed me to signpost some of the biggest
developments in our understanding and treatment of HIV. It has also
given me a platform to share accurate information, such as NAM
resources', he explains.

Matt Hyde also does this well: 'Engaging volunteers, members,
donors and supporters is an essential part of any CEO's role, and social
media allows me to both broadcast organisational messages and help
transform dialogue with stakeholders. It can be used to thank and
champion people as well as dispel myths.'

Engaging

In my opinion, this is the most important, yet trickiest, area of my
social media voyage. Striking a healthy balance between engaging
while avoiding being overly drawn into long-winded, time-
consuming, back and forth conversations, is key. A quick comment
or view on a pertinent issue or post, a heartfelt thank you, an answer

to a question or an encouraging 'like' can all serve a useful purpose in developing engagement and relationships. If people want more than that, I suggest they DM or email me.

Gail Scott-Spicer, CEO of the Kings College Hospital charity, is an active social CEO who says that Twitter is a great way to keep connected. She explains thus:

> You can have a direct one-to-one conversation with people who care about your cause, your charity, your world. As a CEO there is a risk of disconnection with beneficiaries as you rise through the ranks – social media gives you the chance to have that information direct. It can be an early warning system – of change coming, of things going wrong with your charity or your people, of reputational risks increasing.

Sarah Hughes, CEO of the Centre for Mental Health, agrees with this sentiment and is a strong advocate for engaging supporters on social media: 'It's one of the most, if not *the*, most powerful communication tools we have. It is no longer OK to think you can duck it. I am particularly amazed at how easily it breaks down barriers.'

Finally, perhaps an undervalued and underrated benefit is one outlined by James Blake: 'It can provide the ability to appear as a human being, not a CEO!'

Taking the plunge

Being a social CEO can open up a world of opportunity. Kate Lee, CEO of children's cancer charity Clic Sargent, has a simple view on whether CEOs should be embracing social media. 'Stop seeing social media as optional – it really isn't,' she declares. 'If your head isn't above the social media parapet it is probably in the sand.' This is a view held by many social leaders who have decided to take the social CEO plunge. Many say it has now become an important element of their leadership of the organization.

According to Matthew Hodson, social media has not only helped to get people talking about a traditional taboo subject (AIDS), but it has also brought other benefits: 'As a result of my social media work, I have been asked to contribute to articles in the mainstream press and to appear on television.' These kinds of media opportunities are ones that small charities often struggle to achieve. Twitter has given Matthew a direct means of communicating with his stakeholders and others who are interested in the issue.

Caron Bradshaw fully recognizes that the world is becoming increasingly digital and has a much simpler take on things when I ask her why she is active on social media. 'That's like asking why I communicate with people,' she tells me. 'A CEO's role is to be connected and to build relationships. Social media is just another channel that supports that.'

If that's the case, I am often intrigued as to why so many charity leaders are unsure (or reluctant) about dipping their toe into the world of social media. At a recent conference organized by the Association of Chief Executives of Voluntary Organisations (ACEVO), there was an enlightening debate around how CEOs could/should use social media. There was a healthy mixture of views in the room, with the following being some of the most interesting insights:

- Some charity CEOs feel they are now almost being 'judged' if they are not active on social media. One CEO eloquently compared it to similar pressures that new mothers can sometimes face around whether they should breastfeed or formula feed their children.

- Some individuals have strong personal reasons for not wanting to be 'visible' on social media. One CEO from a domestic abuse charity I spoke with called for greater understanding about why some CEOs may wish to stay clear of social media. Professional and personal boundaries need to be respected.

- Time is probably the most common reason cited for not engaging. One CEO told me he has 'enough to think about without trying to find the time to worry about or be distracted by taking part in social media'. He went on to tell me 'that's what the digital team are paid to do'. This is a very naive view in my opinion, but it is important not to forget that social media is something that should be used to support and enhance the work of a CEO, not to take over it. Let's not forget that social media doesn't run the organization.

- Concern over abuse, trolls or being directly or unfairly challenged in a very public forum (which can also be picked up by journalists) also concerns some. John May is very open on social media explaining that 'people get to see the real me'. He feels that is both a benefit and a challenge, telling me he has been described by a number of people as being a bit like Marmite.[2] 'The fact that I'm not a faceless figure, protected by a PR team, means that people will decide quickly whether they like me (and by extension the cause) or hate me.'

My own experience of some of the negative sides of social media played out a few years ago when I was the target of a troll. At the time I was leading an organization through a significant period of challenging change, and someone anonymously decided to begin a very personal attack around the decisions being made by me and the Board, as well as posting their views on my leadership of the organization. I dealt with it as follows:

- I tweeted one early response saying I was interested in their views and was very happy to meet and discuss. After that I had no further public interaction, although there were times when it was hard not to rise to their toxic bait. Clearly, they wanted to lure me into an online engage but, in my experience, there are no winners in pointless tit-for-tat postings and it would have given them further unhelpful oxygen.

- I informed my chair (who was very supportive) and kept him fully up to date with any further posts.

- I asked my digital manager to keep a watching brief in social media spaces and update me on any further posts. However, I couldn't stop myself from a quick regular check on any new posts that they might be spouting off.

- Finally, it was important to remember that in the greater scheme of things, this was nothing other than an unhelpful distraction. Many people have to put up with far more challenging trolls and issues in the social media space! Eventually it just went away.

Matt Hyde is also aware of some of the pitfalls of social media. He leads an organization reliant on 160,000 volunteers giving up their valuable time day and night. He is quick to remind people that 'you don't lead and run an organisation through Twitter, but you are available 24 hours a day and anyone who has a view of what you're doing, or a complaint, can reach you directly'. He strongly suggests that you need strategies in place to deal with this potential open door. 'It's probably not the best use of a CEO's time to be your organisation's customer services department,' he sensibly adds.

A growing movement

Since the heady days of my first tweet, I have been on a constantly evolving journey – and I am continually learning. I'm delighted to have seen growing numbers of charity CEOs fully embrace the social media age – we are all learning from each other. Helping it along the way has been a tremendous initiative called the 'Social CEOs Awards' which since 2013 has championed and celebrated the excellent work of many charity social CEOs.

The Awards were the brainchild of digital consultants Zoe Amar and Matt Collins. They set up the Awards as a way of shining a light on those who were doing the best job. It has been self-fulfilling, helping to show the value and some of the pitfalls of being a social CEO. Without a doubt it has also helped to raise the standard across the board. 'We believe strongly that charity CEOs have a duty to represent their cause online,' says Matt, who is the Managing Director at Platypus Digital. 'Colleagues, supporters and stakeholders all sit up and take notice when a charity leader shouts loudly about why their charity's work is important and what they believe needs to happen.'

Matt goes on to point out that those who are most active on social media typically tend to be the leaders who invest in digital in their organization. By that reasoning, CEOs who embrace social media as part of their own leadership journey also seem to be more aware of, and act on, the wider opportunities that digital brings for their organizations.

Ignore that at your peril I say.

In their words – top tips from social CEOs

John May, CEO of The Duke of Edinburgh's International Award: 'Dive in. Be yourself. Post often. And not exclusively about work.'

Matt Hyde, CEO of The Scouts: 'Be yourself, be honest and authentic. Inject some of your own personality into what you are tweeting and set clear boundaries in your own mind about how much of yourself you want to share with others.'

Gail Scott Spicer, CEO of the Kings College Hospital Charity: 'Go for it! Follow and listen first then take little steps as you develop who you are and how you want to express yourself. After alcohol, step away from social media!'

Caron Bradshaw, CEO of the Charity Finance Group: 'Be yourself. Don't try to over-engineer what you say. Don't be reckless.'

Kate Lee, CEO of the Clic Sargent: 'Think about the things that are of interest to you – competitor organisation CEOs for example.

Follow them to see what they do. Note which tweets really catch your interest and question why. Try to tweet at least once a day.'

Matthew Hodson, CEO of NAM: 'Be authentic. Be interesting. Be kind.'

Sarah Hughes, CEO of the Mental Health Trust: 'Follow some people you admire, a mixture of styles so that you can get a sense of where you might feel comfortable. Be clear about what it is you will use the different platforms for.'

James Blake, CEO of the Youth Hostel Association: 'Take the plunge! Seek advice from others both on who to follow and how to balance your time and input. Be aware of its power and its dangers.'

Matt Collins, MD of Platypus Digital: 'If you're a charity leader, then you definitely have people who want to hear from you. You just have to believe that and get stuck in.'

15

The insurance sector

Jack Salzwedel

In 2008, when I was president of American Family Insurance, my company commissioned Harvard University to conduct a business review case study. The report portrayed us as a slow-moving, staid company lacking innovation and creativity. It questioned our ability to develop a need for urgency and change.

That stung.

The fact that this news was delivered at the start of the Great Recession made it even more challenging.

We took that report to heart, and made significant investments in our people, our infrastructure and our future. We have an invigorated strategy focused on building an enterprise with new business models and service models responding to changing customer expectations – all strengthened by an innovative company culture.

Employee engagement is at or near an all-time high. Customer satisfaction is at near record levels. We've partnered with start-ups in adjacent industries, placing bets on where the future of insurance is heading. Our marketing and advertising programs are considered best-in-class. Revenue is growing. We are among the leaders in the insurance industry.

Compared to a decade ago, American Family has a different culture and strategy now. Today, American Family Insurance is a *transformed* organization.

We started this shift during the early days of social media. American Family was a social media pioneer, not only the insurance industry, but in corporate America.

We launched our brand's social media presence, which quickly earned awards for content excellence and innovation. And we activated a large network of agents on social media, allowing them to connect with customers through social media, with content and training support that was revolutionary in our industry.

The transforming power of social media

How do you go from being a very late adopter, in a late-adopting industry, to moving up to the point where you're in a pack leading the way? How do you engage employees to change corporate strategy? How do you build the culture you need for your strategy?

Of course, a number of factors are in play for my organization: leadership, board support, agent and employee commitment, better focus, investment in technology and key business initiatives. We've brought in people with marketing, innovation and technology experience who have not been afraid of bold changes. That moved us from being a slow follower to, in many areas, *leading the way*.

We used social media as one of catalysts for change during that time, recognizing we had the opportunity to move quickly and get ahead of the competition. We embraced social media as a brand, and I embraced it personally.

From those early stages a decade ago through today, American Family has been nimble and thriving in an ultra-competitive industry – in part because of our approach to social media. It has bolstered our employee engagement and customer outreach. It helps us recruit better. And yes, social media has helped me find my leadership niche.

I believe my use of social media has helped propel the success of our company. It's helped me be a better leader, while connecting with a wider audience than any other communication tool available to me.

Be a better leader

One thing that has really surprised me about social media is that I could be good at it. It's easier than I imagined.

At the same time, I'm surprised by how many leaders are *afraid* of social media. Too many don't feel they have things anyone would be interested to hear, or they think it's a waste of time. Those leaders haven't thought through their own voices or have become too concerned about what they might say. Quite frankly, too many leaders let these fears stop them from trying.

After being active for eight years, I believe it's vital for CEOs to embrace social media. As leaders, we must show others we understand the impact it has on how people communicate and connect – to know how it affects our companies' relationships with customers and employees.

We must also be nimble and be able to grow and change with society and technology. Social media can help accomplish these things. It can also save time by helping us do things more quickly than in the past – from simple stuff like consuming information to more complex tasks, such as identifying new and emerging leaders.

I've overcome some pretty common fears associated with being a high-profile leader in this public space.

You're going to need help, but you also should get comfortable with technology and the tools of the trade. There are new ways of gathering and sharing information, new ways of communication and new ways of showing how we live. *Embrace them.*

It's also a disruptive time for people leading organizations. A leader or CEO used to be able to rely on face-to-face meetings or hard-copy memos to provide direction, inspiration, supervision or training.

During the last ten years, that has shifted. Today, we have a tremendous opportunity to supplement face-to-face meetings and more traditional leadership styles and tools in the workforce with these advances.

Social media is built for this type of leadership.

Employees especially look for you to inspire them, drive their engagement, help them focus on company goals – and listen to them. Your people have plenty of options, and the best ones find it easy to jump to another company, especially when they're dissatisfied with their leaders or their employers. Simply stated, social media can help you be a better leader for your people.

Find your voice

Social media is an integral part of our business today, and its impact extends far beyond being a marketing channel. I started my Twitter account in 2009 because I wanted to be part of the conversation. Today, we have thousands of employees and agents who use social media to connect with me, and each other.

Good leaders won't ask anything of others they aren't willing to do themselves. That includes using social media. My company (and by extension, me) had to be willing to use social media to lead by example. If we're asking insurance agents and our employees to use it, we must show them how to do it effectively.

I've asked my organization to embrace innovation and technology. We emphasize trustworthiness and transparency as two of our core values. Social media helps me exemplify all of these in one spot.

Whether you're a small business owner or CEO of a major corporation, *talking* is how you'll build relationships with people. As CEO, you're building relationships to help people understand your vision and who you are as their leader. As a business leader, it's about making connections so you're top of mind with potential customers.

When I think about communication and leadership, I think about the great leaders I've been around, and the ones whose books I've read and whose talks I've heard. Truly great leaders have these remarkable traits we all want to learn from, but they have some vulnerabilities, fears and weaknesses, too. They recognize shortcomings, and they're actually willing to share.

I also think about a mentor of mine, former American Family executive vice president Darnell Moore, who told me this: 'Find your voice. Be heard.' As CEO, your opinion matters. Speak up! Not every idea or every concern you share will be acted on. But speaking up can help your team correct – or avoid – poor decisions or poor execution.

As CEOs, we're also expected to fill more of the leadership gap left by society when it comes to effecting social change. According to the 2018 Edelman Trust Barometer, 64 per cent of people want CEOs to lead change rather than waiting for government.

Finding our voice as CEOs – and using social media to share it widely – is more important than ever.

Engage with your people

Social media allows you to build trust – and make connections – with people you may not necessarily be able to meet in person. This is especially important for CEOs, who likely have employees, customers and business partners spread across a building, a city, a country or the world. Social media can close those gaps and shrink the world.

Being visible leads to more frequent and closer digital relationships. You could almost call them *friendships*. I agree with others who say that, as a society, we've loosened the definition of friendship, and these *digital friendships* fit those new parameters. We pay attention to each other, we are concerned with each other's lives and we develop these connections that might have taken weeks or months of lunches in real life to cultivate.

If a CEO is going to have productive relationships with employees, social media is essential. These authentic, online conversations help employees feel more engaged, too.

My organization encompasses around 20,000 people – employees, agents who are independent business owners and the employees of those agents. How many of 'my' employees will ever get to meet me face to face? How do I have hallway conversations with thousands of employees half a country away? With Twitter and LinkedIn, I can build connections with those faraway employees and develop *digital friendships* that can be rewarding later on and close the gap of geographical distances.

If you want your employees to feel emotionally invested in your vision for the company, show you trust them. Show they have your trust by sharing your vulnerabilities, and they'll be more willing to follow you because they trust you as much as you trust them.

This willingness to share helps me relate to people on an empathetic level, because people are willing to share with me as well. If people see me as a human being, and not an executive automaton, they relate to me better. And when I see people as real people and not just names on a roster, I relate to them better.

As CEO, you are the main ambassador of the company. You are the *chief communication officer*. And communication is a two-way street. A few years ago, there were more layers between me and everyone else, and there was no direct feedback on what I was saying. We communicated with customers and employees in different ways; we were more formal when communicating internally, but more informal in how we talked about our brand externally. Social media has eliminated those layers between me and my employees and customers.

Create a real-time culture

How do you share news today? Through email, phone or in-person conversations? These twentieth-century communication tools are inefficient and sometimes ineffective for today's leaders. Social media's power and value come through its immediacy and efficiency. A social CEO can share her thoughts in real time with a wide variety of audiences.

The time I spend on Twitter is one of the most enjoyable parts of my day. Not only do I get news more quickly, I also get to connect with people from my company and community. The whole 'This will be interesting and fun and will help the company' argument always wins out over 'I can't put another thing on my plate'.

If you manage it correctly, social media can actually take things *off your plate*.

Every day, using social media gives me confidence that I'm involved with what's going on in my company, my community and the world. I'm not just a name you read about in the news. I get to be more present with our workforce than if I never used social media. Our employees and customers get to hear about the direction we're going and our plans for the future.

Social media is also a powerful tool for foreshadowing or breaking company news, or for supporting advertising campaigns. Our communications and marketing teams often work with me, suggesting relevant content I can share with our employees, our customers or even the media.

If you believe you need to innovate quickly – CEOs like to say if you're not innovating, you're going to die – you need credibility within the organization, and people need to trust your vision. Years ago, the CEO didn't need to be seen as driving innovation or allowing people to learn from their mistakes. But these days, we must be nimble and lean and be able to grow and change with society and technology – what Jay Baer and Amber Naslund, co-authors of *The Now Revolution*, call 'a real-time culture'. (At American Family, we use lean principles and focus on rapid innovation to accomplish this!)

If you're not seen as pushing forward with momentum, there's a real risk to the organization overall. That's why it's important for CEOs to publicly display the tactics *behind the strategy*. If you're not seen as pushing for the next big thing, how are you going to get your team to do it? How are you going to get everyone to move it forward?

Social media can expand the inflow of knowledge and data; improve how you share that knowledge, data and more; connect with and identify emerging leaders in your organization; *and* save your time in the process. As CEOs and business leaders, we can learn a lot just by listening to our communities – not just our shareholders, but customers, employees, hometowns and industries. I get to figure out what is top of mind for my community, and I talk about those things. That's revolutionary for me and my company.

Get help

Surprisingly, 61 per cent of Fortune 500 CEOs still have no social media presence at all, according to CEO.com. You can't do this alone, so find someone who can help you launch (or perhaps relaunch) your social media presence. This person – or people – can make a huge difference to the way you approach social media.

Getting help in social media starts by finding an advocate in your organization. This should be someone you trust, but who also understands social media deeply. Most importantly, he or she needs to understand *you* and your style and won't be afraid to nudge you – frequently. This *social media advisor* will need to push you, but not so far out of your comfort zone that you quit using the medium five minutes later.

An advisor is also important because – let's face it – you can't know everything there is to know about the platforms. They're always changing. Your advisor can help with things like administration, setting up lists to follow or perhaps sending post ideas.

Be vulnerable enough to accept help from someone who's probably younger than you.

For eight years, I've relied on people at my organization who fit these qualifications – Tom Buchheim and Michele Wingate. They have held social media leadership roles at my company. They understand our brand, people, culture and strategy. And, they know me enough to be comfortable giving candid feedback about what I'm saying in social media and how I'm saying it.

Tom and Michele also understand social media – really well – and have been using it effectively both personally and professionally for years. Having people like that around is most important for any leader, especially if you're worried about not getting it right the first time. I've strengthened my voice by using social media, and by working closely with my team, they've come to understand my voice.

Plug into your brand

As CEO, you must be part of a larger communications strategy for sharing company news or supporting marketing campaigns. As my advisor, Tom works closely with our communications and marketing teams, keeping me in the loop on news and events, and part of the content mix, if appropriate. If it's worthy of more thought, we'll turn my ideas into a longer-form post for LinkedIn or my blog.

It's all about transparency and making my job as *chief communication officer* easier. In my role, I certainly see and hear about a lot related to my company – and I'll share that when it's appropriate. But I can't know and see everything. So I rely on others who are listening and plugged into *everything*. Tom is especially skilled at filtering this river of information into something I can review and decide what's sharable.

Plugging into your brand is an important step in becoming a social CEO. And because you are in a leadership position, your personal social media presence can be seen by anyone – including the media, customers and the competition. It's why you need processes in place to monitor conversations about you, in case something should arise that requires a response.

As a social CEO, you're also *part* of your brand. People will find you. They will ask you for help – finding a job, resolving a customer-service issue, pitching an idea or product. It's not your job to answer them all, although some CEOs can – and do. But it is your brand's job.

I'm plugged into my company's processes, so those folks get the help they seek. Our care centres are empowered to respond on social media if someone reaches out to me for help. They're listening for this and are in the best position to answer questions and solve problems. It's vital as an insurance company that we track and document these conversations, too. Our corporate security team also monitors conversations about me and our brand – looking for potential threats and keeping our people safe.

What's next?

Social media has come so far, so fast. In some ways, the sky is the limit. The current networks may go away or change, and new ones may rise to take their place.

But just as they have for thousands of years, people will want to communicate with each other. They don't want to be yelled at, dictated to, talked down to or completely ignored. They want to connect with other people, not faceless corporations. They want real communication and connection, not marketing messages. They seek authentic leadership.

No matter what happens to the channels we're using today, even as they evolve and change, we still need to communicate with people in the way they want to be communicated with, on the channel where they can be found.

Social media may have changed *how* we talk, but it hasn't really changed *what* we say. People still want to laugh, learn, empathize, be informed and share. Social media helps me be part of that, and I hope it can help you be part of it, too.

16

The social enterprise sector

Jan Owen

To affect social change, you have to believe that change can happen, believe you have something to contribute, believe that collective action and bringing people together matter and believe in conversations that elevate the voices of those who don't have a platform of their own.

Social change is not for the faint-hearted and neither is social media. Finding your voice in the cacophony of white noise is a core twenty-first-century skill and capability for those wishing to influence public policy, drive conversations forward and affect social change.

As the CEO of the national, for-purpose, Foundation for Young Australians (FYA), I am asked daily to connect meaningfully and often with our stakeholders, partners and participants, to build value-adding collaborations and embody the spirit of our organization.

With a diverse audience of millions, spanning the length and breadth of the country, social media is a key way to stay connected, responsive and relevant.

Beyond this, we live in a digital age where many significant conversations and influencers are active online. Long gone are the days where a CEO could send out some media releases and wait for a press call to engage in the conversations that matter to their organization. Today's CEOs must proactively invest, monitor and participate in online conversations, not only about their organization but also about the broader world in which they operate, to be seen as credible and reliable.

This is especially true for CEOs of NGOs and for-purpose organizations today. According to the 2018 Edelman Trust Barometer, we are facing a society increasingly distrustful of NGOs and leadership, with 84 per cent of people expecting CEOs to inform conversations and policy debates on one or more pressing societal issues, including jobs, the economy, automation, regulation and globalization.

I joined Twitter in May 2011. Before that my social media use was limited to Facebook, opinion pieces and traditional media via mainstream news or current affairs.

So, how does a CEO who's new to social media become good at it? Where do they begin when it comes to new media as a tool for connecting with such a significant audience?

For me, FYA's brand and content strategy is a driving force behind how I approach being a social CEO.

Using social for good

FYA has been around in its current form since 2000. Over this time it has evolved from a strategic philanthropic funder to a leading research, advocacy and social enterprise organization.

With a mission to grow and support generations of young changemakers to create a more sustainable and equitable future, FYA works with thousands of young Australians each year to unleash their potential. We also work with the people and institutions who make decisions that impact young people's capacity to thrive and create the world they want to live in, from educators and parents to policy makers and employers.

We do a lot of things face to face at FYA, but with 79 per cent of Australians checking their social media at least once per day according the 2018 Sensis Social Media Report, online is where we can engage with the largest, most diverse audience.

FYA now brings together one of the largest digital communities of diverse young people in Australia, with a social media community of over 150,000 on Facebook and Instagram, as well as regularly over 50,000 visitors to our website each month. Our audience of educators, policy makers, parents and employers are made up of over 30,000, mainly from Twitter and LinkedIn. As CEO of FYA, my own Twitter and LinkedIn accounts also have close to 30,000 followers.

It wasn't always this way. Four years ago, FYA had a social media community of 4,000 and under 7,000 visitors to our website monthly.

So, how did we get here?

A strong community can only be built and maintained when there is a shared vision among your team about why you want to reach your audience, who you are specifically trying to connect with and how you are going to connect with them. A lack of clarity regarding any of these questions within your team will lead to confusion for your audience and, ultimately, disengagement.

At FYA we want to see young people at the centre of decisions that impact their future. We also want to engage those who support young people to ensure they are equipped to navigate and thrive in a rapidly evolving world.

To do this we had to get better at putting our audience at the centre of our strategy.

Probably the most critical decision at any point in time is this: What strategy do you need to adopt for what result? Information dissemination is different to driving conversations, and different again to running campaigns. Once your strategy is clear, then choosing which platforms support this approach and measuring the impact are important.

People, platforms and posting

Put your audience at the centre of your content.

This sounds obvious, but previously our site and social media were simultaneously trying to reach young people as well as our partners and funders. By trying to cater for both, through the same channels, we weren't really hitting the mark with either. Young people didn't feel like the content spoke to them, while stakeholders wanted to see how we brought our strategy to life online – recognizing the agency of young people, putting their voices at the centre and hearing about how they could help to do the same.

At FYA we are fortunate to have an extremely talented group of young people leading our digital work. This includes creating our content as well as building a network of young contributors. Our most popular content are articles written by young people from within this network, proving you don't have to be a writer or journalist to create content that resonates.

We put young people at the centre of discussions for our stakeholder audience too. But the topics are tailored towards their interest in FYA's research and policy work around the future of work, education, learning and social entrepreneurship. Similarly, we have a team that creates and curates content from young people and those working with them who can share insights into what challenges and opportunities young people are experiencing at school, at work and in life.

My role as a social CEO

This is where my role as a social CEO comes in – with targeted thought leadership, including a monthly blog and responsive opinion pieces shared across my professional channels. This content has been a mechanism for raising issues, flagging solutions and testing new ideas that demonstrate the organization's understanding of the broader context in which we operate. The engagement around this content has been consistently strong – in fact it is some of the most highly read content on our website.

Once you've got the right content, you need to choose the right channels so that it reaches your audience.

At FYA we have channels primarily dedicated to our youth communications (Facebook, Instagram and YouTube) and separate channels predominantly focused on communicating with our stakeholders (LinkedIn and Twitter). As I primarily talk to our stakeholder audience, I use Twitter and LinkedIn a lot, posting at least twice a day, if not more often.

Importantly, I don't have multiple personal or professional accounts for Twitter or LinkedIn. I don't utilize these platforms for my personal views or self-promotion, but only to elevate FYA, our mission and the conversations we are seeking to have by engaging in real-time online discussion about the issues which affect and inform our strategy.

I aspire to be present and to assert my own voice and personality rather than just churning out the same content or that which our official FYA channels share. While it's important to support this content and be connected to the organization's 'why', it is also important to join live conversations, respond to people in real time and be prepared to demonstrate my own expertise and lived experience.

This clarity of purpose is key to enabling me to stay in the FYA wheelhouse and makes it significantly easier for me to do the bulk of my own posting and responding. My team support me by running campaigns like my 'One Incredible Young Australian a Day' which I started in 2018, but I make the vast majority of posts myself.

Cutting through the noise

Once you've got your channels straight, how do you make sure your content cuts through and has an impact on your readers?

Our community is looking for expertise, insights and the voices of young people.

Giving young people a platform where they can have their say and voice their opinions, with little censoring or direction, and broadcasting their views to allow them to speak for themselves across our channels are core to our mission.

'It begins with me' is a well-known social change adage. As CEO, this means being willing to stand up for what FYA (and young Australians) believe in.

In 2015 FYA received funding to convene the Safe Schools Coalition of Australia to support young LGBTIQ+ people, based on a model from the United States which we piloted in Victoria with Monash University. Much has since been written about the ensuing political and media storm which followed this critically important teacher, parent and student information and training 'opt-in' high school initiative.

As the storm raged, FYA stayed consistently on-message about the purpose of this critical program – writing articles and blogs and giving media commentary, despite the avalanche of attacks on the program on social media directed at specific individuals, in emails and commentary on our websites. We stayed the course and worked incredibly hard behind the scenes to ensure the initiative was not shut down during a long and sustained attack. It took fortitude not to fold under the pressure and play into the firestorm created through the media.

What kept us going was knowing that some LGBTIQ+ young people could literally die without this support in their schools. To play into the hands of the critics would be indefensible and mean allowing the program to be defunded two years before the contract ended. It was the right thing to do. We, and our six state and territory partner organizations, received some criticism for this, but we also learned an essential lesson regarding when to use social media channels and when not to.

By 2017 when a postal survey for marriage equality was called, FYA joined the call across all of its social channels for a 'yes' vote. As the co-founder and convenor of the Safe Schools Coalition, we knew that young people care about, and want to live in, a society where all people are treated equally.

With a short video and blog post about why we supported marriage equality, we demonstrated FYA's commitment once again. The content was well received – but beyond that, we were able to continue to stand with our community of young people.

More broadly, not just organizations but young people themselves, from around the world, have found their voice and platforms to build powerful social change movements online.

The recent courage of Emma Gonzalez, Greta Thunberg and Jean Hinchcliffe are no exception. Being under eighteen years, these three extraordinary high school students took a stand to make the world safer, more sustainable and more equitable. These young women led school students onto the streets of cities across the globe to protest inaction on gun laws and climate change.

They've had an impact. Not only on millions of their peers around the world but also in changing hearts and minds and emboldening others, across all generations, to stand up for what they believed in too.

Politicians and powerful institutions were enraged and told them to be quiet, to go back to school and study, but these students were awake to the facts.

With over two million social media followers between them, Emma and the March for our Lives movement gained a larger following than the NRA (National Rifle Association) in just a month. Young climate change movements globally have engaged with millions in dozens of countries. Social media has provided a generation of young people a voice and platform for the issues they care about which cannot easily be shut down.

Sharing creates exponential social change

We are privileged to have many of Australia's brightest and most inspiring young social entrepreneurs, innovators and changemakers in our FYA community. There is nothing I like better than to share the journeys, learnings and wins of our community, partners and stakeholders. In turn our community of young changemakers, innovators and activists share their stories, campaigns for change, outcomes and achievements across our channels.

The compounded effect of sharing other people's content, starting a conversation and adding value and insight is immeasurable. It is at these times that I feel I am in a deep, rich and connected ecosystem of collaborators, rather than some echo chamber bouncing the same ideas around four walls.

The learning journey never ends

Like most CEOs, I am still learning how to utilize these tools for change for the most impact. I have definitely made plenty of mistakes.

For example, when I engage in issues beyond our remit at FYA or my previous CEO roles and experiences, no matter how interesting they are, they rarely gain traction. Also, I don't always seem to be as humorous as I think I am. I have come to learn that staying focused and strategic is key to success.

However, I am never afraid to enter unknown territory where I can learn and gain new social media skills.

Some skills are transferable offline to online – and not just by utilizing 280 characters succinctly. Being a regular facilitator of groups and communities in my working day makes it a great deal easier to engage with a variety of communities. I have been asked to host Twitter groups and Twitter conversations connected to television or radio shows, and we have often live-streamed launches and presentations and the 'In Conversation' events we hold with experts at FYA. These are all fantastic ways to listen, learn and engage in live conversations.

We all know video is huge and I have utilized it across Twitter and LinkedIn recently with my young shadow CEO, Sherry Rose Bih Watts, reporting on our CEO days together and providing commentary from special events and conferences – all with great feedback.

As a for-purpose, nonprofit organization, FYA doesn't have unlimited resources at our fingertips to execute our work, so our team members have had to be efficient, clever and quick learners. We've adopted and are continuing to work on building a culture of testing. We recognize that with an online world that is constantly changing, what worked for us one month might not work the next.

This is particularly true when you think about the volatility of using third-party platforms like Facebook, Twitter and Instagram, where you are essentially a user not a controller of the audience data you've paid to build. You also have no control over the sometime baffling changes that occur on these platforms or how users will and won't engage with them. We're still working through our strategies about how to navigate this constant change.

With a world of choice at social media users' fingertips, creating cut-through and building a community is work that takes time, resources, commitment, adaptability, genuineness and consistency.

FYA has come a long way in the past few years, but we still have a long way to go, more people to reach and many more ways we can improve our efforts – from influencers and user-generated content to thought leadership across the organization. The social learning journey really never ends. But there are a few essential ways to ensure success.

Five tips for success:

1 Put your audience at the centre of your journey. Make sure you capture what your audience wants to read, see and hear in any of the content you create and distribute.

2 Choose your channels carefully. Pick platforms that you understand, that your audience uses and that are easy for you to be responsive on.

3 Be present, responsive and authentic. There's no point in a CEO pushing out exactly the same content in the same way as a faceless organizational channel would. Make sure to embed your personality, otherwise what's the point?

4 Be consistent. Stay connected to your why. Stick to your niche
   areas of expertise and to the values of your organization at all
   times.

5 The journey is never over. Watch and learn from others.
   Be willing to test different approaches and keep changing
   the content and delivery because social media is constantly
   evolving.

17

The environmental sector

Mark R. Tercek

Before becoming CEO of The Nature Conservancy (TNC), the world's largest environmental nonprofit, I was an investment banker on Wall Street for twenty-four years. As you can imagine, this was quite a transition.

In the business world, I kept my private life to myself. In the environmental space, I found that people wanted to know more about who their leader was. This was a big adjustment – and one that social media helped me navigate.

I'm still very much a novice, but here are few lessons I've learned as a social CEO in the environmental sector.

Building an authentic voice online

In my job at TNC I was encouraged to share some aspects of my personal and private life, similar to the way political candidates do.

While most of my social media posts addressed environmental challenges, I tried to weave in details about my travels, occasional family news and personal interests. I'm told that my colleagues and TNC supporters enjoyed following along with what I was reading, where I was traveling and what topics were top of mind.

At the same time, I've learned that sharing personal details online can cut both ways. For example, I'm a vegan. I've never really chosen to be an evangelist on the topic because people want to make their own choices about their diets. But some of my colleagues encouraged me to be more open about this part of my life.

For some environmentalists who were unsure about a conservation leader who hails from Wall Street, sharing this information on social media increased my credibility. But other key constituents, including farmers and ranchers who are working very successfully with TNC to improve sustainable agriculture practices, got miffed. I can understand and respect both perspectives, but in the end, I've found sharing this information helpful to building an authentic voice online. Just because I'm a vegan doesn't mean I don't appreciate the farmers and ranchers around the world who are doing their part to sustainably manage land and feed the world's populations. Two things can be true.

Watching out for nuance

Whatever field you're in, you probably deal with some touchy subjects on occasion. Some controversial topics, especially nuanced ones, aren't well suited for social media. That's a lesson my team and I learned the hard way.

For example, I once penned a thoughtful blog about genetically modified organisms (GMOs). It was very balanced. The blog made the claim that we should let science be the guide on whether or how GMOs can effectively and safely be used. My colleagues and I then shared the blog on social media.

As it turned out, this was unwise.

The blog generated a flood of vitriolic hate mail, which isn't very useful for an NGO's reputation or its valuable staff time. What's more, the hate mail was inconsistent with the contents of the blog. It appeared that the letter writers hadn't read or understood my argument.

Another challenge I've faced is using humour. I tend to make very dry jokes, and sometimes people take them too seriously. I once shared a picture online of my daughter sitting on the set of the David Letterman Show, thanks to a friend who had access to the production set. I wrote a cheeky caption about her becoming the next host – and received many serious inquiries and notes of congratulations about my daughter taking over for the King of Late Night.

Spreading the word

Of course, social media is also a good tool for raising awareness for your mission. We can all write blogs, speeches and books – but people are busy, and there is a lot of messaging out there. Social media is a good tool to let people know what your organization does that makes you proud.

I was very fortunate. I had a great job where I came to work every day with excellent colleagues and inspiring partners to address the biggest challenges humankind faces.

But the work itself was hard. Take climate change. It's the biggest threat to the planet, but greenhouse gas pollution is invisible. That makes it hard to convince people about the urgent need to act.

What's more, there is an unwillingness to address the root causes of climate change, like dependence on fossil fuel energy. The solutions require massive transformations of the economy. Creating change at the scale we need will take more people and more resources on our side.

Thanks to social media, environmental organizations like TNC now have a low-cost way of communicating with huge numbers of people. The trick of course is being creative in crafting your messages to stand out from the many voices online. I found that talking about science in terms of real projects with tangible outcomes could be very compelling. You can't overdo the wonkiness if you want to engage a lot of people. Plus, social media gives you good, instant feedback on what gets traction and what doesn't. Try something new, see if it works and if it doesn't you can delete and try again.

By the way – it works the other way around, too. I used social media to support peer organizations and shine a spotlight on important, but sometimes less visible, work. And it also helped me learn what was going on with other organizations and leaders. For example, if I was invited to speak at a conference, I could follow along with the event hashtag to catch up on the events of the day and what people were talking about. I also recommended to my colleagues that they follow a small number of thought leaders in their field – this is a great way to discover important news and analyses as they happen.

A valuable tool

When it comes to social media, I'm still very much a beginner. But I found it a good way to connect with my colleagues and TNC supporters, stay informed and highlight the important work of TNC and other great peer organizations. I can't imagine a CEO in any business not wanting to use social media as a tool for advancing their organization's mission.

Five tips for social CEOs in the environmental sector

1 Don't engage with trolls online – only in person. In real life, I believe it is very useful to meet and discuss with your critics. I always told my colleagues that our critics were often our friends – they wanted the same outcomes we did, they just wanted it done a different way. When we did have a chance to meet with these people or organizations, we often ended up learning something new. (And they learned from us too.) However, I have not found that this approach works on social media.

2 Be positive. There are a lot of mean-spirited, glib critics on social media – and a lot of room for more positive voices. When you come across good news that should be shared broadly, support it.

3   Be wary of humour. Not everyone has the same sense of
    humour. What's funny to you might not be funny to someone
    else.

4   Support lesser known causes – and don't pile on. This is
    especially important if you have a big following. You can
    retweet smaller or lesser known organizations that are doing
    good work or tag journalists who are doing important, tough
    reporting. And resist the urge to pile on celebrity tweets
    where your voice will be drowned out.

5   Grab attention. Recognize that social media is competitive,
    and your posts need to grab attention. One thing I tried to do
    was ask for feedback from colleagues on what they thought
    would work best.

18

The start-up sector

Katie Elizabeth

What's trending today? Who do I need to engage with? How can I offer more value to my followers and connections today? Am I doing enough to stay at the top of my social media game?

These are some of the business-as-usual questions that cross my mind nearly every hour of the day. I've found it imperative to be connected socially when in a leadership role, especially leading a Silicon Valley start-up.

As you can imagine, being the CEO of a Silicon Valley start-up is difficult as it's one of the most competitive markets in the world, with statistics showing that only about 10 per cent of start-ups succeed. If the CEO is active on social media, though, it makes their company more likely to join that 10 per cent.

Social media is one of the most dynamic and valuable resources today. Each platform lets people voice their opinions and engage with others. Careful listening can provide valuable insights into market trends, uncover new opportunities and (most importantly) help you understand your customers better. Furthermore, today's consumers expect a level of communication and transparency from CEOs that can largely be accomplished through an active social media presence. The lack of that, however, communicates to millions of current and potential customers that you don't care about what they have to say about your brand.

A company's brand presence is also dependent on the social presence of the CEO. Research shows that 80 per cent of the customers are more likely to trust a company if the CEO has a strong social media presence. Additionally, more than 70 per cent people feel that a CEO's social media activity helps with effective communications, building better relationships with employees and customers, boosting the social presence of the company and enhancing profitability and customer acquisition.

Customers aren't the only ones who expect to be able to engage with you online. It has been found that employees feel more engaged at work and consider the CEO to be a better leader if she or he is socially active. Moreover, 80 per cent of employees prefer working with companies that have a strong social media presence, which all but requires that their CEO be socially engaged.

Given that over 2 billion people access social media via mobile apps each day (and growing by 1.6 million users per day) opportunities for your start-up abound when you engage socially. When you are in start-up mode, success or failure can be determined by whether or not you are a social CEO. It's that important.

As a start-up CEO, I can attest to the fact that social media has benefited my company immensely. I met my lead investor and a key advisor via Twitter. I've also met countless amazing professionals through LinkedIn and Twitter. All have helped my start-up grow.

In many ways, building a successful company is about building relationships; social media has helped me to accomplish that. But that doesn't mean that being socially active has made it easy.

Be it marketing strategies, launching a product or customer acquisition, it's tough in the fast-paced, ever-changing world of Silicon Valley. Almost everything depends on you – success or failure. Here, business waits for no one and success depends entirely on you bringing your A-game, being timely and never dropping the ball.

When you are a CEO of a growth-mode start-up, you need to personally thrive in order to bear the weight of all the responsibilities. You work ten to eighteen hours a day, nearly 365 days a year, for years on end to achieve success. You carry on each and every day, working to make your start-up even more successful than it was the day before. Meetings, partnership calls and so many other to-dos fill your days. You are driven, and you put in your all 100 per cent of the time.

You know social media is important – and so is being highly responsive. What if that 'bing' on your phone is the message you've been waiting for, the one confirming the largest contract your company has ever seen? 'Shouldn't I check it to be sure?' You pick up your phone and check every time because your dedication to your work and your start-up demand it of you.

You carry a heavy load each day. The interests and investments of numerous people are at stake in your success or failure – from early employees and investors to advisors, friends and family. It is something you take with you daily, carrying the responsibility of having so much riding on your decisions. Buckling from the pressure is not an option. And to stay steady, you need to be connected with other like-minded people who can cheer you on, offer advice and guidance and help create a sense of camaraderie. Social media is one of the very best ways to accomplish this.

I have discovered that finding people like me on social media is easy – people as driven and as passionate about what they do as start-up CEOs. The challenge, though, is making time to connect with them, or with anyone else for that matter, and creating relationships while the world of your start-up moves at breakneck speed. When I connect with other start-up CEOs, I insist that they don't ignore social media. Beyond the personal benefit that helps a leader thrive personally, these platforms are, in essence, your customers, potential employees, investors, partners and almost everyone that could benefit you and your company.

Without a doubt, social media is one way to execute great leadership. As we all know, a pillar of strong leadership is effective communication. In today's digital world, that means social media. It is the means to make your mark, maintain a presence in important circles and keep you in the know amid the myriad of things going on around you. It is a way to engage with friends, family, clients, prospects – pretty much everyone!

The opportunities and benefits of being a social CEO in a start-up are limitless. You can meet investors, advisors and future team members on various platforms. Through simple interactions and connections, you can form lasting relationships with peers anywhere in the world. You can also build your industry and community presence, in turn attracting more customers and prospects to your start-up. Even opportunities to meet great team members are significantly increased simply by being a social CEO.

But, here lies the problem: when you're already at full tilt with every other part of running your company, trying to keep up with social media can feel futile! On the other hand, if you're not on social media these days, you'll get your lunch eaten by those who are. People related to your start-up value and expect the transparency, communication and presence it provides. It helps to meet those expectations by being an active and engaging social CEO.

My approach to being a social CEO is this: I dive in and enjoy myself. I appreciate the interactions and the learnings I gain from the vast number of connections and interactions that I have. The potential it has to grow my start-up and help me meet new and interesting people along the way is beyond exciting. I see it as a very effective way to connect with other like-minded people, make new connections and stay on top of what's going on.

I will admit that, when the workload becomes intense, I've pushed social media to the bottom of my priority list. It is hard to keep up with when there are always so many pressing concerns on your plate. During those times, though, I still make sure to have content going out as best I can, even if I'm not quite as active in engaging in dialogue. As I mentioned earlier and will do again, the value of the transparency, communication and presence it provides for a start-up CEO is astronomical.

When time is tight, for my most important relationships, I am always sure to still like, comment, retweet and otherwise engage with them. This is very important to maintain healthy connections and relationships, so I make it a priority to do so as much as I can, no matter how busy I get. I also make sure to never be half-way absent for too long – otherwise my online presence will suffer, which can affect the start-up that I work so hard for each and every day. Social media is an integral part of being a start-up CEO, and I never take that for granted.

Five tips to help start-up CEOs better utilize social media

1   Be your real, genuine, authentic self. Nobody likes to get catfished, whether it's by 'a date' or by 'the CEO' of a company. Let your genuine self be known and value the insight only you can have. Trying to be anything other than yourself is just setting everyone up for disappointment somewhere down the line.

2   Don't be afraid to reach out to people cold on social media. Some of my most valuable relationships began this way. Many friends, peers and team members have started from connecting on social media and are based almost entirely on interactions and connections that I continued to nurture and foster. It's a big internet out there – you never know what interesting people you'll meet.

3   Share things your audience will find valuable. While you shouldn't just push content, it is helpful to have a steady stream of value-added content going out. It is what defines you from everyone else, makes you memorable and makes you stand out from the crowd. Be timely and relevant with the content you choose and use it as a means for your connections to get to know you better. Pull from your personal experience and use supportive online sources to provide your network with content that is interesting, engaging and directly helpful or relevant in their lives. Make sure, though, that the content always represents your real, genuine, authentic self.

4   Engage, engage, engage. Content is great. It gives your
    connections a means of getting to know you, your interests
    and your views. Content, though, is not enough. What
    is more critical is nurturing meaningful relationships.
    Engagement is the only way to achieve this. Have actual
    interactions with other people as your real, genuine, authentic
    self – don't just push content. When you engage consistently
    with people on social media you can start to build your
    network and remain top of mind if they ever need what your
    company offers.

5   Be respectful, be nice. Be ever aware and follow proper social
    media etiquette. Be respectful of your connections and value
    them. Treat others as you wish to be treated. It means replying
    to people, commenting, liking, following. Always treat your
    connections with kindness and respect. Something to always
    keep in mind is that social media is about interacting, not just
    about posting.

Being a social, start-up CEO is difficult. It is hard, hard work, but it
plays an integral role in the success of your start-up. Social media is
immensely valuable to you and your company and is a necessity in
today's world. Take it from me – a highly passionate, highly motivated,
highly caffeinated and chronically connected social CEO.

19

The education sector

Mary Curnock Cook

This chapter is mainly about Twitter. I signed up in 2010, shortly after being appointed CEO of UCAS, the UK's centralized admissions service for higher education. As my first summer at 'mission control' for the university clearing system[1] got under way, the head of communications told me proudly that we were trending on Twitter. I decided to sign up, using my full name (@MaryCurnockCook) as my Twitter handle.

For several months I 'lurked', only browsing my feed infrequently, but getting into the habit of checking what students were saying about UCAS as one of my weekend tasks. It was a revelation. I had what felt like a finger on the pulse of student sentiment throughout the agonies and ecstasies of the university application cycle. It was a huge help in an organization which wasn't then used to thinking of students as customers.

Then a few things happened which drew me in.

First, I was at a National Union of Students (NUS) event and, on the train home, my email lit up with notifications from Twitter. I was getting virtually live feedback on the speech I had given earlier in the day. I opened my feed with some trepidation, only to find mostly positive comments and a bunch of new followers.

Next was a nerve-wracking moment on the evening before clearing opened in 2013. I was briefing the then universities minister, David Willetts, on the statistics for entry that year and he was nervously hoping for news that applications had bounced back following the dip that had accompanied the rise in tuition fees the previous year (they had). Midway through the briefing, someone came in to tell me the devastating news that the UCAS website was down following a DDoS (distributed denial of service) attack. My calm response of 'Please let me know as soon as service is restored' belied my sense of impending doom.

The next day, as universities confirmed students' places, we needed to be ready for a spike in traffic to our website, which could get up to five or six hundred hits per second at its peak. This was the worst possible moment for our website to be down. Happily, the service was restored in a little over an hour. As I got back to my flat, tired and relieved, I tweeted: 'Denial of service attack on ucas website this evening. Service back on. Hackers 0, UCAS 1'. This was not popular with the tech teams back at UCAS who felt I was inciting the hackers to try harder. But I was rewarded with retweets and outraged support on Twitter – and that felt good.

The third and still the best thing to happen to me on Twitter occurred as I unwound from a busy week after clearing in 2014. It was a Friday evening and I was playing tennis when my phone starting pinging almost continuously. A poor signal at the tennis club meant that I couldn't check what was going on until I got home. A sense of dread spoiled my game as I wondered what I might have done or said to enrage the Twitter community.

It turned out to be the now-legendary letter turning down an application to study at 'Hogwarts University'. 'We regret to inform you that your application cannot be processed at this time due to the fact that it does not exist', it said, continuing that 'your handwritten grade sheet claiming top marks in "waving a stick about", "wearing a pointy hat" and "watching Paul Daniels[2] TV specials" sadly is not suitable for submission.' The image showed a convincing image of the UCAS letterhead with my recognizable signature at the bottom. Brilliant! And it was being shared by hundreds of people.

Among the Twitter responses were several journalists and commentators trying to find out whether it really was written by me. I sat at home in my tennis kit wondering how to respond. I wanted to join in with what was, after all, a very funny prank while also acknowledging that it wasn't me who'd written it. Eventually I came up with: 'Of course it's genuine – silly muggles. In fact it's magic....'

Cue hundreds more shares, including a few rather po-faced ones from people who clearly hadn't read Harry Potter and thought I was trying to claim credit. In one weekend my followers climbed from about 300 to over 650 and the press picked up the story as well. I loved it.

These three incidents taught me a lot about Twitter. First, with social media, 'public speaking' means speaking to the public rather than just the audience – and that sets a much higher self-censoring bar when extemporizing and answering questions. Second, sharing operational pain and challenges can draw people into your world in a positive way. Third, a bit of humour is never a bad thing.

The Hogwarts letter now does the rounds on social media every summer in clearing season and the reputational afterglow that UCAS got from it was almost entirely positive. As one Twitterer put it: 'Brilliant letter from UCAS @QuantumPirate > haha! UCAS have a sense of humour! Who knew :-)'.

As my confidence and understanding of Twitter grew, so did my tweeting, retweeting, commenting – and followers. Twitter became my early-morning newsfeed – the quickest and best way of finding out what was going on in education and what was in the headlines. Gradually increasing the number of journalists, wonks and commentators that I followed gave me a good sweep of my sector. There wasn't much that I missed.

Engaging with Twitter in this way also helped me work out how to increase my own presence by watching what worked for others. Timing is important and it seems that most people hit their Twitter feeds at about 8 o' clock in the morning. However, now that Twitter has introduced the 'in case you missed it' feature, getting active early in the morning is less vital, but you can still see a pattern of retweeting as people visit their feeds at the beginning and end of the working day.

On social media, as in other areas of life, you reap what you sow. Being generous with your 'likes' and retweets is often repaid by people who appreciate the signal that you have noticed their contribution.

A couple of times I used Twitter to combat negative press stories, getting my rebuttal out before most people had even seen the relevant article. Contacting sympathetic supporters via direct messages on Twitter and asking them to retweet helped build momentum for the response too.

It's important to clarify that I always composed my own tweets. My emerging Twitter voice was definitely me, not my corporate communications team. I never put 'views my own' on my profile as many do in what seems to me to be a fairly meaningless way. I was scrupulously careful, however, because while I was tweeting under my own name, I clearly had a responsibility to my organization and our customers as the CEO.

Although UCAS is not a government organization as some people think, it does run a public service and therefore has a role in the national infrastructure of the education system, including working with government and sector agencies. I therefore avoided any party-political stances on Twitter and still like to think that my politics are opaque to my followers. Neither would I have ever overtly criticized government policy or shown any preference to a particular university or course. This might sound obvious, but I am still surprised by prominent players in the education sector seemingly willing to display their political leanings. I prefer to keep that to myself to ensure that I don't colour future dealings with government when elections change the scenery.

And it goes without saying that tweeting while even slightly under the influence of alcohol is not a good idea. Taking care over what you say and how you write it is a must, especially if, like me, you cringe at the typos that stay on the record long after you touched the wrong key. For this reason, I've given up on live tweeting at events. Perhaps I'm getting old, but I find I'm just not good at getting the tweet spot on in the heat of the moment and often end up missing the event or speech in question while trying to perfect the message. Better to take a few photographs that you can use after the event to accompany better thought through messaging.

There is also a lesson for over-hasty tweeters to learn from Toby Young's[3] evisceration by Twitter when he was announced as a board member for the new higher education regulator. What you say on social media platforms *is* public, and almost impossible to remove from the record.

There is a lot of quite mundane stuff shared among professional communities on Twitter and I am still learning how to stand out among the thousands of tweets landing on everyone's feeds. Using original language helps. Retweeting an article with a 'this is interesting' comment usually doesn't get much traction. My preferred approach is to shorten the URL of an article or report, and then to copy and paste a pithy quote from it.

I'm a fan of the Mark Twain quote: 'Sorry this is such a long letter; I didn't have time to write a short one', and I enjoy the challenge of fitting everything I want to say into the character limit. I don't like shortening words in 1990s text/SMS style; this might have been a pragmatic approach when we all had phones where the numbers had to be pressed the requisite number of times to type a letter of the alphabet, but there's no excuse today – it just looks unprofessional. That said, I occasionally allow myself to slip in an ampersand when searching for a couple of characters to bring a message in under the limit.

Twitter's new functionality to develop threads is helpful too, allowing you to comment in more depth and add images. A snipping tool is a must for energetic tweeters, allowing you to quickly copy and paste bits of text, interesting graphics or charts to enliven your tweets. These appear as images on your tweet and therefore don't eat into your character count.

Occasionally I 'bleet' something. This is a cross between a blog and a tweet. You type a longer comment in Word, use the snipping tool to turn it into an image and then tweet it, adding logos or images to make it more visually appealing. It's not quite as perfect as a corporate tweet template but has an ever-so-slightly home-made feel to it which I like to think adds to the authenticity.

Alongside education-related tweeting, I occasionally drop in something personal. It's good sometimes to show some personality and to be prepared to reveal something of the real you behind the professional image. My banner photograph is of my three children and I change my profile picture reasonably frequently. Sadly, it's a fact of life that including photographs of my dog (especially when he was a cute puppy) often gets more shares than messages I have worked hard on to put across an interesting stance on something to do with higher education.

Adding some warmth to your social media presence takes little effort and is often repaid with returned warmth in your community. I was overwhelmed with kind messages when I announced my resignation from UCAS on Twitter at the end of 2016. I also had a similarly warm response to quite a personal and reflective thread that I tweeted on my sixtieth birthday – alongside a triumphant photograph of my 60+ Oyster card[4] for free London travel.

Now that I have stepped down from executive life and have a portfolio of non-executive roles, the Twitter community has become even more important to me. Without the platform that a national CEO role gives you, without an office and colleagues and without a treadmill of meetings and events to attend, it is easy to feel out of touch and isolated. I have a little more freedom to state my views now that I'm not the CEO of a national organization, but I continue to tread carefully in political waters, especially as I am on the boards of a public sector organization, a university and several charities that work in the public sphere.

Without the public interest that comes from a high-profile role, I have to work harder to stay current and relevant on Twitter. A busy week can leave me absent from the platform and it shows in the statistics. There is also a circular relationship between the time I am able to give to reading articles and reports and the quality of my tweeting. The two go hand-in-hand – you have to have something to say, after all.

Since stepping down from an executive role I have also paid more attention to LinkedIn where, despite having thousands of links, I have never been particularly active. Now I have to keep an eye on it for messages from people who don't know how to reach me at my kitchen table office. I'm beginning to see the benefits of sharing and blogging there too.

But, in the end, I'm definitely a Twitter person. It's part of my professional life and I treat it with respect while also recognizing that having a few thousand followers does not mean that anyone's that interested in my views. It can be something of an echo chamber and I'm often reminded that many people in the education community see my tweets without commenting publicly. All the more reason not to get too obsessed with the online response and remember always that it's a very public forum.

20

The B2B technology start-up

Oliver Lawal

A week ago you had a nice office, meetings, deadlines, a full inbox and a nice pay-cheque. Your personal brand was enhanced by the corporation you were part of. Now you're sitting with a dog at your feet, next to a laundry-laden exercise bike. You did it. You started a new company. You secured a URL and set up social media accounts. Now your task is to use your personal brand to enhance your new business. To translate your ideas, passion, experience and personal gravitas into marketable credibility under the banner of your new business-to-business (B2B) technology start-up.

Standing out

Social media claims to have the advantage of allowing everyone to have an equal voice. The reality is that you will need to be more than equal. You will need to stand out.

The most obvious use of social media for a technology start-up is to engage with potential customers, because you need them to become actual customers. You're desperate to start showing some sales revenue to your investors, so you find interesting ways to explain how awesome your product is. You make sure everyone knows what problem you've solved, what your value proposition is and that the lead time is less than two weeks. You're fast, you're nimble, your product is so much better than what's currently available.

That's all good. No harm done. However, with a new company in the B2B space, no matter how good your widget is, it's unlikely that you will have brand credibility or volume of followers that will move the needle on sales revenue. So, while you won't do any harm, you may be limited in your scope of good.

Effective social media use is about telling your story. Of course that includes telling it to potential customers, but there are other target audiences for your story too. These include the following:

- Investors. If you want to move out of your basement office, you're going to need investors. Whether it's Uncle Jim, or Venture Capital Mary, you need to attract them and keep them attracted. Targeting product messages to investors (and potential investors) is good to show confidence in your development progress, but you can also show elements of your hard work and dedication. Early morning images of a well-used keyboard will play well, but posting pictures of a new car to someone that just gave you a large cheque should be avoided. It can seem odd to target a message to a tiny group of two or three people, but in the early days, these are the most important two or three people in your world.

- Employees. Attracting and retaining the best and brightest will be aided by a solid social media feed. In much the same way as investors are, these internal stakeholders will be buoyed by you publicly celebrating their achievements and sharing them with those they care about most.

- Supply chain. Credibility is the key here. As a new entity you are trading more on hopes than on history. It's important to show the future value in partnering with you.

- Competitors. Trolling is a very effective way to get in someone's head. I personally avoid directly commenting on a competitor's thread in order to avoid drawing other's attention to them. However, targeted messaging that will be clearly understood by them can draw benefits. Announcing achievements can be demoralizing to them. This is a double-edged sword – if you're not careful you will motivate them into action. So careful application of misdirection should be used. For example, if you're keen on entering market area A, then following twelve companies in market B will throw the best cyber-stalker off the scent.

Telling your story is important. Maintaining the lead voice in your market is important. However, it's also important to understand that your 'market' is more than paying customers. You're marketing to all resources: investors, employees and suppliers.

The benefits of being a social CEO

Being active in a field of discussion and having a consistently honest voice help others to trust you. This is particularly important when communicating within the B2B sector, because you're dealing with fellow engineers and designers. They may well be in need of your product, but will often have a natural scepticism.

Direct communication as a CEO can pay real dividends as it's unlikely that the established technology providers will have meaningful communications from their CEO. Your ability to show a clarity of message, vision and credibility will be an advantage. Following and taking a sincere interest in other, more junior members of your industry will set you apart.

Avoiding exaggerated claims, negative messages and technical errors is critical. Having a consistent, sincere tone is key, as this is the beginning of a potentially long business relationship. Also, developing content marketing that emphasizes education over direct selling is important. White papers, web pages, patent references, journal articles, case studies and infographics are all great tools. Assuming you're a CEO with a technology background, it's important that you stay closely connected to the content generation. This will ensure content quality is maintained and changes based on constant market learnings can be reflected.

My approach

Authenticity might be an overused term, but it's needed. I know a fellow CEO who has posted no content apart from pictures of exhibition booths and golf outings in two years – not a single share/ like/comment/engagement outside of that. For him that might be authentic, but it's not even remotely creative. As such, for me, authenticity needs some caveats.

My personal approach is to maintain an online voice that reflects a high-level vision for the whole organization: the problem we're solving, with a special product, made by amazing people – while still being involved in the daily details. In other words, I try to show variety between the strategic and the tactical.

On LinkedIn I keep posts, shares, likes and so on strictly on-topic to my industry sector, albeit being mindful of all stakeholders: end users, distribution channel, direct customers, consultants, academics, regulators, competitors, employees, suppliers and so on. On Twitter I feel more open to reflect my true work-life balance and show involvement in family, hobbies and community, in addition to the variety of work-based engagements. I stay away from party politics but feel it's important to engage in conversations related to specific issues that relate to my industry.

It's important to remember you are talking to people. Some tend to forget that in the B2B sector. These people are interested in your technological product advancements – which are achieved by your team of real people – so celebrate them. By having a focus on people and their achievements you can better connect with others who are ultimately their peers.

Challenges

I spent twenty years developing a career in a specific industry sector, moving across three continents, taking increasing levels of responsibility in executive positions with publicly traded companies. My interactions with others were judged by a combination of the corporation brand and the job title on my business card. I was a good-sized fish in a good-sized pond.

In many ways starting a new company made me a minnow overnight – even though my knowledge, passion and experience remained unchanged. I needed to lean more heavily on my personal brand to develop the new company brand. Then, as the new company expanded, I needed to constantly re-adjust the lens to focus onto the growing team and their achievements.

In the B2B space new, disruptive technologies are often met with resistance. The time and cost to integrate a new technology is often significant, and it's not uncommon for bold claims to be less than bold in the cold light of day. Therefore, overcoming adoption-inertia from a customer requires patience. In addition, the conventional technology providers will have greater credibility in negative messaging to prevent adoption (or delaying until they think it will work for them).

Educating an industry on the benefits of this paradigm shift takes incremental effort which can seem juxtaposed to the instant pace of social media.

It's important to establish and maintain a position of thought leadership. However, creating meaningful, high-quality content over the long periods of time needed to impact B2B new technology can be exhausting. I have seen many well-intentioned blogs or newsletters extend little past the first few issues. Viewing a social media account or company news web page that hasn't posted in twelve months probably does more harm than good for a new technology company. It may be necessary to teach new employees (or yourself) that have come from large organizations to treat messaging as a marathon and not a sprint.

It's exciting to develop something new – and introducing it to the world is exhilarating. However, in the small world inhabited by a B2B technology start-up company, any new introductions will probably be watched more closely by competitors than by potential customers. Additionally, the integration and scale-up time can be long; therefore in developing a new technology platform, I have found that it can be tricky to balance the showcasing of your own product's capabilities without motivating competitive challenges. This should not be a reason to stay in 'stealthmode' indefinitely, but being thoughtful about the timing and level of detail of sharing is important. I have found that placing 'teasers' to allow you to screen detailed product information can be effective.

Five social media tips for B2B technology start-up CEOs

1   Patience. It will take twice as long, with double the effort, to achieve half the reward. It will still be worth it.

2   Quality over quantity. A large content pool and network is nice, but quality content and a quality network are better. Ensure you have a balanced network of all relevant stakeholders.

3   Balance focus with pivot opportunities. Make sure everyone (customers, investors, employees, supply chain, distribution channel) has a crystal-clear understanding of what you're doing, but don't paint yourself into a corner should a pivot be required.

4   Leverage your membership or leadership of other organizations, whether they be industry-related or not. As the CEO of a small organization it's important that you show greater depth and capabilities.

5   Be creative. Not all your social media interactions will work, but the more creative you are, the increased chance you have to be interesting to others. Learn from those that work and those that don't.

21

The tech sector

Paul Frampton Calero

There are few roles more exciting than being a CEO in a fast-growing, early-stage tech business. There are equally few roles more exhausting. There are always a hundred more things to do, and the pressure is constant to complete every project faster while successfully delivering new proofs of concept.

Peter Drucker famously said that 'culture eats strategy for breakfast'. Even more so than in a corporate environment (where I worked for two decades), this is true in a tech start-up.

Culture is the one thing that can't be plagiarized by another company and is the single biggest differentiator between good and brilliant teams. When you are a young business, culture is also the difference between failure and success. Few commentators have perfectly encapsulated what culture is, but for me it is the combination of the following three things:

1   How a company behaves when the leadership team is not in the room.

2   The invisible glue that bonds departments together as one
    single team.

3   How and what employees share and express externally (at
    events, but now increasingly on social media).

Core values

Prior to running Tink Labs, a travel tech start-up, I ran a large
advertising group called Havas. There I instigated two initiatives
designed to maximize the second and third points. The first was a
biannual, all-staff celebration of what the company had achieved,
hosted at The Odeon in Leicester Square, London. Twice a year we
shared the remarkable (but also the failures) versus our strategic plan,
inviting talent from every department and level onto the stage to
share their successes.

The second initiative actually came into its own at these company
events. This was the hashtag #havastogether: two simple words that
linked our core value of togetherness with our master brand.

Too often, companies complicate and confuse both internally and
externally by communicating too many values. In my experience,
employees struggle to recall more than two. This simple social-ready
phrase #havastogether was therefore designed to be a shorthand for
why the group was different to every other – namely because our
teams genuinely worked together collaboratively with a shared vision.

I then encouraged talent across the organization to use this
hashtag wherever they witnessed something that represented that
togetherness. Soon it became a palette from which talent in London

and across the world selected different shades and colours to express their own interpretation of togetherness.

At the biannual celebration at The Odeon, #havastogether always trended on Twitter in London, demonstrating the power of mobilizing company culture through a simple badge of honour. If you search for the hashtag today, I'm confident it still has momentum as an expression of the company's culture.

The tech start-up challenge

I was always proud that in Havas there were forty or fifty core supporters who would regularly like and share content on social but, in reality, this was a fraction of the workforce. Nothing could therefore prepare me for the power of a similar strategy in a start-up environment.

In Tink Labs, togetherness is one of our core values, as is turbo (otherwise articulated as Done is Better than Perfect) – and I'm thrilled that a whopping three quarters of the team are regular social advocates for the business.

When you get culture right in a smaller business, the impact is quite remarkable. This is likely where the term 'rocket ship', often used in the start-up world, comes from. When people align their own purpose with your reason for existence as a business, magic happens!

New leaders

Somewhat ironically, as a direct result of social media itself, today's CEOs must be more customer- and people-focused than ever before.

We're living in a world of radical transparency where faux behaviour – either from an individual or from a company – is quickly outed. That, however, is not enough of a reason to be active on social.

The best leaders exist to serve their talent and do their very best to create the optimal environment so that this talent is able to do the best work of their lives. For me, this service needs to be evident and shared on a daily basis.

Social channels provide CEOs with the opportunity to succinctly express company goals and priorities to both customers and talent. Social media enables the CEO to be much more accessible and closer to their workforce, most of whom will have limited day-to-day contact or insight into their leader.

Internally, social media will reach a wider cross section of the workforce than any staff meeting or email. Nothing can replace face-to-face contact, but social complements this by offering greater frequency and regular engagement. In a world where leaders need their talent to follow and believe in their strategy, this is essential. Talent can only follow if they are aware of and understand a leader's vision.

Social media is unique in that it offers tools for leaders to express their thoughts, perspectives and beliefs openly and authentically on a daily basis. What's more, by 2020, 50 per cent of the global workforce will be millennials – and within this demographic there is an increased expectation for leaders to be more accessible and authentic.

Show your human side

I also believe in the powerful ability of social media to show the human side of a CEO – and different platforms do this in different ways. Instagram and Snapchat provide the opportunity to showcase the 'outside-of-work' self: family, interests and passions. Twitter and LinkedIn lend themselves to the sharing of powerful insights, thoughts and perspectives on key topics. Employees want to know more about their CEO and never has there been a better opportunity for CEOs to both connect and demonstrate proximity and vulnerability.

When it comes to the tech sector, humanity can be a powerful tool. Often the product and technology drive everything inside a start-up – but storytelling is an essential weapon in getting external audiences to engage. I am a big fan of Simon Sinek and his focus on the 'why': 'People don't buy what you do, they buy why you do it.'

I like to think of social media as both a live focus group and advocacy at scale. Observing what people are saying or not saying about your brand brings huge customer insight – if there is no conversation then you're not doing enough to spark one. Similarly, when you do share content that people love, they will share it for you organically.

While you also need a sprinkling of paid social media to reach the big numbers, it always starts with brilliant storytelling that engages, inspires or entertains. When done well, it's not unusual to generate new business leads – some call this social selling, which I find a tad blunt. For me, if you share interesting perspectives and engage in interesting conversations, people will want to interact and work with you. People buy from people after all, and social media enables people to connect with a much wider network than they ever could in the physical world.

Attracting talent and advocates

In an early-stage tech business, social media can also be a powerful tool and platform for both attracting talent and putting messaging in front of other key stakeholders, including customers, potential customers, the media and investors.

LinkedIn in particular is not purely a place for identifying potential employees but, as it is where most of the conversation resolves around careers, professional development and diversity, it offers the ideal platform for building your company's employer brand.

My personal view is that this should be spearheaded by the most visible figurehead of the business, namely the CEO. A CEO active on social media, regularly sharing the stories that arise from their business, will benefit from an influx not only of engaged advocates but also of talent interested in working for them. As I mentioned above, this makes the business more human by giving it a face and personality. Quantitatively, it will also save thousands in recruitment agency fees as candidates will approach you directly.

Not all plain sailing

While there are so many benefits, being a social CEO is far from easy. It is a big commitment. Having 25,000 followers across Twitter and LinkedIn means that, just like a media outlet, I do feel the responsibility to publish regular and relevant content.

As a genuine social CEO (rather than a CEO on social media), you have a responsibility to engage with your community, which includes responding to incoming DMs (direct messages). Unlike the media outlets of yesterday, social media is not a broadcast medium – it is a community, and much like any community it is those who contribute most and support others who succeed, while those who drown out others will fail. While the number of DMs can sometimes be overwhelming, I always take the time to respond as there will always be gold dust to be found in places you least expect it.

By putting yourself out there you are inviting both comment and criticism. I am fairly outspoken about diversity and gender equality and as a result have received public attacks from certain quarters, particularly men. Over time I have perfected my response, which is not to ignore, but instead to acknowledge every opinion while standing my ground.

The way I look at it, negative comments happen in all walks of life – social media just allows people to more easily hide behind a computer or fake profile. I do like to think, however, that there is more good than bad. Social has after all enabled powerful global connections and given so many meaningful movements a voice and platform to drive change (not least #MeToo).

In summary, I am a firm believer that social media is not just a 'nice-to-have'. It is not a shiny new thing. It should be a fundamental part of every CEO's – and indeed every leader's – daily life. Not only is it in an incredible, organic communication platform, hopefully I've demonstrated that it's also a unique platform for staff and customer engagement, talent acquisition and business development.

Five social media tips for leaders
of tech start-ups:

1   Social helps grow your business – having an active social
    presence will attract talent and customers.

2   If you aren't sure where to start, simply start by following
    others and engaging with their content. They will reciprocate
    and will build your confidence.

3   Define two or three watermarks that you want to stand
    for and structure your content around these. Mine are
    Disruption and Diversity.

4   Be prolific across different platforms, as they reach different
    audiences in different modes. Tailor your content to the
    platform.

5   Don't be afraid to show your human side. The highest
    engagement I've received was when sharing thoughts on how
    to balance being a father and a CEO.

22

The municipal sector

Charles Pender

Being the mayor of a small rural city in Atlantic Canada has many challenges, differing only in terms of magnitude when compared with other larger, more urban centres. No matter the size of the city, municipal leaders all deal with the same assortment of issues, from roads, water and waste management to providing community policing and fire protection, encouraging business growth and balancing annual budgets – all while attempting to keep the majority of taxpayers happy.

Of course, every city and every town have its peculiarities, and if you live on the edge of the North Atlantic as we do in Newfoundland, then you also have to deal with 15 feet (5 metres) of snow every winter, mixed with the occasional hurricane force winds, rain and mid-winter thaws – and the flooding that results.

Mayors are often the community leaders closest to the people they serve. They deal with residents face to face, day to day – especially in smaller towns and cities. They are the face and the voice of the city or town they lead.

Embedded in the community – listening and engaging

I've always been involved in my community, one way or another, and have loved every minute of it. Being the mayor of a small city has allowed me to experience some pretty amazing opportunities over the years. I've met performers, artists, well-known politicians and royalty, and have participated in federal, international events and meetings, including having the privilege of placing a wreath at the Newfoundland War Memorial to commemorate the ninetieth anniversary of the Battle of the Somme. I have many fond memories of these occasions and of the many people with whom I've worked – but the most rewarding feelings come from knowing that I had the good fortune to serve my neighbours and friends in a role that few get to experience.

When I turn on the tap and drink what is some of the best drinking water in Canada, or drive by our new, modern, City Hall complex that houses our library, museum and performing arts centre, or take a walk along the beach of the only city-owned park on the waterfront (that didn't exist five years ago), I'm proud of all I've been able to achieve on behalf of my fellow citizens.

Of course, I didn't accomplish these things alone. As a leader you can have a vision of where you want to go, but if you can't encourage and inspire others that your vision is worth following, then you're going nowhere. Leadership requires that you find common ground with people, some of whom directly oppose you, but who can be convinced that your shared vision will benefit everyone, including them.

This means that you have to develop the ability to not only hear, but also actually listen, and that you consider everyone's opinion as being of value. That's not always easy to do, especially in politics when your opponents are constantly fighting for media attention.

One group that often goes unnoticed in municipal governance is one's employees. We often take these people for granted, but when push comes to shove and Mother Nature is battering your community with everything she has, you had better be certain that your employees are on the job, ensuring the safety of your residents' property and, yes, even their lives.

If there's one lesson that I've learned as a municipal leader, it's the importance of supporting your senior staff and your employees and making sure they have the tools and resources they need to get the job done, safely and efficiently. This means investing in innovation, equipment and training – and it also means, again, listening to front-line workers and giving them an opportunity for input. For me, knowing what you *don't* know is as important as knowing what you do know. A good leader listens to those in the know and finds ways to put their knowledge to use.

Instant communication

An important lesson I learned from my time at City Hall is that people have become more demanding when it comes to knowing what is happening in their community. With the advent of social media platforms like Twitter and Facebook, people have come to expect instant communication delivered directly to their tablet or mobile device.

Luckily for me, one of the things I discovered I was particularly good at was using social media. It not only allows you to reach people like never before but, more importantly, also provides an opportunity for people to reach you directly. It's a tool like no other when it comes to speaking to a targeted audience instantly and, unlike traditional media, it allows you to say exactly what you want to say without the use of any intermediary, editor or filter. It also allows you to get instantaneous feedback, allowing you to modify and update your messages, something which is particularly important in the event of an emergency.

As mayor, you are seen as the person in charge. Even if you have a team of professionals and councillors around you, people consider you to be the face and voice of the community. Your constituents want to know that *you* are listening to them and that their thoughts, ideas and concerns matter to you.

Social media really allows you to keep your ear to the ground to catch issues as they arise, to gauge public interest in an idea or initiative and to provide an opportunity for feedback. Whether it's simply the number of views, likes or messages, if used wisely, social media can tell you what people are thinking and the direction you should be heading.

Obviously, it's not always that simple. There are always outliers who will fight for or against anything, but social media can provide you with a running snapshot of the community mindset and help you respond to their needs and aspirations with much greater clarity.

As mayor I invested an enormous amount of time, energy and intellect in promoting the collective agenda of the city. Once a direction was set, as a council, we needed everyone to be on the same page both internally and externally. Being adept at social media afforded me the opportunity of sharing that vision daily with all those who mattered and who took an interest in what was going on within the organization.

Honestly, in this day and age, it really doesn't matter what you accomplish if nobody is aware of it, so you need to spread the word. If you don't, you'll spend most of your time putting out fires instead of building and maintaining support for your initiatives.

Social media allows us to reach directly into the homes and offices of those who take an interest in what is happening in the city. It allows direct, two-way communication that provides users with the ability to have last-minute information on developing situations as they evolve.

If there is a traffic disruption that will disrupt their commute, a fire or police emergency in their neighbourhood or an unplanned water outage or sudden flooding in an area, being able to connect quickly and spread the word through social media has proven time and time again to be an extremely valuable tool for municipal officials.

I cannot count how many times people commented on how important it was to them to get timely, accurate information that allowed them to make decisions that impacted on their day. A simple Facebook post on a winter morning about road conditions after an overnight storm, for example, proved so effective in reducing the number of inquiries and complaints to city phones that it quickly became a staple of my winter social media duties. And as the information came directly from our Public Works Superintendent to me and then to the general public, people knew it was accurate, unfiltered, up to the minute and reliable.

My unique approach

I had actually developed my own social media following before becoming mayor for the second time. I had a personal blog where I commented almost daily on city issues, as well as my own personal Twitter and Facebook accounts. Each platform allowed me to connect in a different way with followers. Over time, however, I found the blog to be largely redundant as I discovered that most people who were looking for updates were going to Facebook. They weren't always interested in the minutia of the moment, but simply wanted accurate information they could access easily and use immediately.

As mayor I found that using Twitter worked well when posting topical information, when seeking feedback on initiatives or when informing people of something happening at that moment, such as a traffic disruption, a fire or police emergency, a sudden water outage or something that could have a direct impact on a person's day. It was also useful for reminding residents of upcoming community events, new initiatives or public meetings.

Twitter and Facebook are also excellent mediums when reporting live from an event, and as both of these platforms have evolved, anyone can now be the reporter on the scene, as it were. I often tweeted live from an event, posting pictures and videos for those who were unable to attend. Facebook live is another great tool that, if you are willing to put yourself out there, can prove to be a very effective and rewarding opportunity for municipal leaders.

As Twitter is limited to 180 characters (which of course is immensely better than the old 140 characters) I often used tweets to direct followers to a link that provided more information, a news article or a Facebook post. The great thing about Twitter is the back and forth communication that it allows – residents could reach me directly to let me know of a developing situation, ask a question or, yes, even to make a complaint.

Don't get swamped

On a cautionary note, it's important to recognize that the effectiveness of these platforms to communicate directly with residents can become all-consuming. As people realize that they have the power to reach you at any moment of the day or night, on weekends and holidays, without going through official 'channels' – and that you are likely to respond to their questions and comments – people can become increasingly demanding, which means that you can quickly become overloaded. So, it's very important to set limits and personal guidelines as to how often you will respond, what types of comments and messages you will respond to and comment on, or whether you will simply acknowledge that someone has reached out to you and that you have passed the information along.

Of course, like with any tool, you have to hone your skills and make sure that your content is pertinent and speaks to the people reading your posts. That comes with time and practice.

While some of my colleagues liked to comment that I was 'always' tweeting, the truth is that as I became more adept at understanding what my followers expected from me, the amount of time and effort it took to tweet became less and less. I developed a system that worked for me, using Facebook for longer posts about initiatives and emerging issues and acknowledging citizens and employees – always accompanied by pictures. I used Twitter for shorter messages that were more immediate which, again, were often accompanied by a picture to catch people's attention. And, of course, always with the appropriate hashtag to help expand and continually grow my follower count.

I can't emphasize enough the power of social media in helping shape local government policies. As a municipal leader, you know that people want to be heard, they want to know that you've gotten the message and that you will do what you can to help. And if you can't do anything, because of any number of constraints, at least you've listened to and heard them and have acknowledged their concerns, thoughts or ideas.

You are giving them the ability to speak directly to the 'head' of the city, something most people never even think is possible. Indeed, even in a small city like ours, there is a bureaucracy, a system that requires people to call and leave a message so that someone can pass that message along, hopefully to the correct department, and then someone in that department will assign the problem to someone else to deal with and so on.

Imagine the complete shift in power when residents can reach out directly to the person in charge, without going through anyone else, and simply ask a question, raise a concern, point out an issue and get a reply almost immediately. It may not always be possible to resolve the matter, but it's an acknowledgement of their concern – which can be followed up by action, because the mayor has direct access to senior staff and can cut through channels, especially when the matter is urgent – that matters.

This usually prevents the situation from blowing up and allows people to see that you are working on the situation. It also helps limit the 'bandwagon' effect so common on social media, where people jump on a topic and feel the need to have their say, regardless of whether it affects them directly or not.

The challenge of time

The most difficult challenge with social media is staying on top of things. If you are going to be relevant, you don't want your content to become stale – and this of course can place enormous demands on your time. In my case, I spent so much time building followers and developing content that I really didn't realize how much time I was putting into my social media activities on a daily basis.

Given the fact that most of us have a smart phone in our pocket, we can literally be online all the time, which in itself can become counter-productive, as you start to post for the sake of posting, without really delivering anything of value. In my case, I realized that the more time I spent on social media, the more I felt the need to do more and more. At some point I came to the realization that people only expect what you lead them to expect.

So, after taking the time to review my Facebook analytics, I learned when my followers were most likely to be online and timed my posts to reach them when they were actually logged into Facebook. I started to reduce my time spent online, planning Facebook posts to appear either in the morning before people went to work, or in the early evening when they were most likely to be online.

While I always take everyone's comments at face value, I have also learned that it is best not to engage with people who hide their identity or use a pseudonym. The trolls of this world can and will take over your social media life if you engage them. It's just a personal policy that I have adopted, but I have found that people who put their names to their opinions and comments tend to have something worthwhile to say.

Five social media tips for municipal leaders

- Be honest, kind and positive. Remember, it only takes a few seconds to post a tweet, but that tweet will live forever on the internet – it's your reputation that's on the line for everyone to see.

- Take the time to get to know your followers; don't assume you know what they are looking for – that's what your analytics are for. Sometimes it's trial and error, but if people are following, viewing, liking and commenting, then you're on the right path.

- Don't respond to trolls or anonymous posts – they're not worth your time.

- Research, review and reconsider your comments before posting – especially when you are discussing or debating a hot topic. Sometimes what you say doesn't always come across as you intend, especially in the heat of the moment – and that can blow up in your face quickly. I have probably erased as many posts as I have made, but occasionally I have posted something and subsequently acknowledged that something didn't come across the way I was thinking it would. When that happens, be quick to acknowledge it and clarify or apologize as required before the internet eats you alive.

- Don't overdo it – there really can be too much of a good thing. Strive for quality rather than quantity. Posting for the sake of posting can turn people off and cost you followers, so stick to what you know and what your followers want. But at the same time, don't be afraid to toss out the occasional trial balloon, because we all need to take a chance now and then, and who knows where it will lead, who might connect with you or who will be inspired – it might even be you!

23

The travel sector

Tom Marchant

Being a leader in the travel sector often feels like you are walking through a forest of blessings and curses. Blessings in that you get to introduce people to the best experiences that this planet has to offer, curses because you are at the mercy of the constant volatility that rages throughout the globe: currency fluctuations, political unrest, natural disasters, disease, war. The ebb and flow of our planet's daily life as it spins on its axis means the job of leading a company designed to deliver on people's travel dreams is a tricky one.

But tricky is good. It keeps you on your toes, drives you to innovate and forces you to pay attention to emerging trends, shifting passions and new means by which people get inspired to travel and subsequently plan their travel.

No one area better sums up the world of shifting passions and new means of getting travel inspiration than social media.

At first glance social media, and particularly the visually driven social media platforms such as Instagram and Facebook, are seen as manna from heaven for those people operating in the travel industry.

Millions of images, posts and comments shining a light on destinations and experiences act as a fantastic catalyst to inspire people to travel. That's good, right? I think so, but perhaps not for the reason you may think.

The default view of social media being a great stimulant to get people to travel is not always shared by the travel industry. Why? Well, unless you are a huge airline or a supplier who has a monopoly on a particular destination or service that people simply have to use to be able to experience it, you can find yourself at the mercy of the 'do it yourself' attitude that social media has fostered among some travellers. See an image, read the recommendations, book a flight and you're done. Or so they think. People have begun to take a view that they no longer need travel service companies to facilitate their trips, based on the fact that if they can see it, they can just do it.

Now I know, and I would hazard a guess that a lot of other people know (certainly within the travel industry) that this is not how it works. The evidence bears it out. Countless people travel without consulting experts, basing their choices on the 'wisdom of the crowds' on social media – only to find that the recommendations don't always match their expectations, aren't aligned to their passions and are sometimes just plain wrong. Add to that the fact that anyone with half a creative brain can apply filters and tuning to make a place look good, and this all means the 'do it yourself' consumer can find themselves in a world of half-truths and broken promises that were only originally shared for the ephemeral pursuit of likes.

But let me stop my rant there. I need to be clear. I love the millions of images being shared, comments posted and insights offered, because it stimulates interest in travel and increases the desire to see the world and to connect with other cultures – and that is always a good thing.

Importantly, it also creates opportunity – opportunity for my company and me to engage with this audience and establish a voice within this world which positions us as a source of true value, expertise, insight and passion when it comes to getting the most out of a destination.

We use social media to inspire but, as importantly, to convey why and how you should be travelling. We want to make sure that, yes, you do get to stand in that beautiful spot at sunset and to fall in love with the place but, as importantly, that you work with a company that takes you beyond the image. A company that helps you find stories and build connections in a place that will feed the soul and give you memories to treasure for the rest of your life.

So, as a leader in the travel industry, how do you do that? How do you cut through? You need to establish social media authority; you need to garner trust. In short, you need to be more than just a pretty picture. Social media, when executed effectively, is a wonderful tool for building thought leadership.

Conveying your message through compelling (and yes, often beautiful – this is travel after all) imagery, but with engaging copy that clearly communicates the value and insight you offer through your services and why you stand apart, is essential. Why? Because it works.

In this increasingly overwhelming digital world where we are being hit by thousands of messages every day, often from sources we don't know and users who may be bots, the consumer is crying out for someone to stand out. Someone who can speak with confidence, honesty and integrity and help them navigate their way through this manic, murky and, at times, meddlesome world.

How do I and my company do it? Two key instructions always dominate our conversations when looking at our social media approach: (1) be honest and (2) be human. I often think that point 2 can't happen without point 1 as, after all, isn't honesty a fundamental part of what it means to be human?

Why are these important? As referenced earlier, the social world is a tricky one, full of dead ends, fake posts, fancy filters and auto-text. It can foster a disenchanted nature among users who end up not trusting/believing what they see. How to combat that? Be honest. Speak in a language that is conversational, is informed and gives people a genuine take on something. Don't be scared to show fallibility or call something out if it doesn't feel right. Most importantly, be honest with yourself about what you are putting out there – that it truly represents you and your business.

People want to know who you are, see how you think, understand what inspires you and what passions of yours lie outside of the boardroom. They want more than sales pitches and advertorials. They want to know what makes you tick and why they should follow/believe in what you and/or what your company does. This doesn't mean trotting out motivational quotes each morning (if anything turns me off social media it is that). Rather, it means not being scared to show who you are and bring point 2 into the mix – be human.

I like to blend what I share between developments at work that excite me (this could be new product launches, activities my team are working on – people love to see what is going on under the bonnet

– partnerships, topics that we are scratching our head over, etc.) and also what my other passions are.

I am a parent and I love exploring the world with my wife and child (be careful not to overshare though). I don't share this stuff with an agenda; it's simply who I am and what I care about. I share other passions too: food, sport, literature and more. I simply want to show what I care about, what I am passionate about and, in turn, what fuels me and in turn my business.

I don't sit down with an annual content strategy; I simply live by the rules of being honest and being human through my social output – and I am fortunate that this resonates with people and also aligns with how we approach our social output at Black Tomato.

Yes, people love to see top ten lists (and there will always be a place for that) but equally, followers of Black Tomato get really excited when they get to meet the people behind the brand and the people they will meet when travelling. It's not filtered; it's not dressed up; it's just honest, passionate people sharing their love and interest in what they do. You would be amazed how easily that resonates with audiences and builds a following.

As a company, we have a presence on all the major social media platforms, but where we most enjoy sharing – and where we feel we have the opportunity to best communicate what we believe in – is Instagram. The rise of instastories has enabled the company and me to lift the lid more effectively on what we do and, alongside this, we are embracing Instagram TV and its abilities to bring beautiful content to our audience. Our in-house film production team are constantly travelling to film and share stories routed in being human and being honest. The impact they have when shared with our audience is profound.

Being a leader in a business that embraces this social world can be an extremely satisfying experience. At the same time, if you hide behind glib statements and filtered images, then it can be a disingenuous one that ultimately may lead to you being caught out. And who wants to build a business based on smoke and mirrors anyway? People are looking for ports in the storm. Informed ports in a social storm, and that's the approach we take. A very necessary one in the world of travel.

Alongside being honest and being human I would add the following three tips for any budding leader wanting to embrace the social world:

- Build trust.
- Let people under the bonnet.
- Keep talking – don't ever, ever go quiet.

Follow those tips and you will be on your way to building a social presence that will resonate and support and grow with you long into a successful future. It's working for us and I hope it will for you, too.

24

The small business owner

Samantha Kelly

Hard beginnings

I was always a hard worker, but when I was younger I drifted in and out of jobs, not quite settling anywhere. I had temporary positions as a receptionist, a waitress and lots of sales and customer-service roles. I loved dealing with people but wasn't so great at taking orders from a boss! I always made great tips when I was a waitress as I knew how to talk to people and offer excellent customer service, always going above and beyond what was expected of me.

But somehow I was never quite happy staying in one place for long. I was adaptable and a fast learner, but doing what I was told was never my strong point. I was feisty, stubborn (at times) and not a very good listener. I was also very sensitive.

When I had my first daughter I wasn't in a good relationship, so I left and went off on my own. I lost a lot of confidence and didn't think I had anything to offer and ended up relying on social welfare. I didn't quite know what I wanted to do – and as many lone parents can relate to, I didn't have the childcare in place to get out and get a proper job.

Eventually I divorced and got married again and had my second daughter – but again I was feeling unfulfilled and wanted to do something, but didn't know what. What was my purpose in life? I was a bit lost. I felt like a failure and I was also very lonely. It was at this stage that I started relying on alcohol (although I've now been sober for over ten years).

Since that difficult time I slowly began to realize that I *did* in fact have useful talents and something to offer the world.

This new mindset started in 2011, when my father passed away. It was this that really pushed me into action. My dad was a real 'Del Boy',[1] always thinking of ways to make us millionaires! We came from very humble beginnings, and my dad worked really hard as a painter and decorator. He had that great skill of being able to talk to anyone in a room – from criminals to the poshest people – and make both laugh. He had friends from every walk of life. Devastated when he passed away, I entered a 'life is too short' and 'you only live once' frame of mind, thinking about what I'd done with my life so far. I decided it was time to do something – but I still didn't know what that something was.

My second marriage had broken down, my second daughter was about to start mainstream school (she is hearing impaired with a severe language delay, so I was on a carer's allowance) and I was about to hit the Big Forty. All my ducks were lined up in a row – with nowhere to swim.

A new opportunity

Then my eldest daughter came to that awkward milestone of having her first period; I felt sorry for her and went to the shop to buy her some sort of gift or starter set. To my surprise, I found that there wasn't such a thing. Right there and then in the supermarket aisle, I decided that I would create a gift box for everything a young girl needs, and Funky Goddess, my first business, was born.

I had no business experience, never went to college and had no money – and didn't exactly have a great credit record with the banks either! But I just did it. I researched online, sourced everything I needed and decided to promote it on social media as I had zero marketing budget. My sister put me on Twitter and said, 'Off you go'.

Despite having little experience with social media, I discovered that I was pretty good at it when it came to marketing Funky Goddess. I was talking to people and building relationships even though I didn't realize that's what I was doing. When the girls were in bed, I was talking to people on Twitter, learning as much as I could about it and social media in general. At this time, I also appeared on the Irish version of *Dragon's Den*[2] and my profile soared through media appearances (let's face it, periods were a bit of a taboo, so the media loved it). By this point, I had gained a following of over 5,000 people.

The investment I needed from the show didn't materialize, but I was determined to succeed. I needed to turn a profit though, so in the end I made the uncomfortable decision to shelve Funky Goddess and get out and earn some money. I put up a post on my Facebook page telling my customers that I was selling Funky Goddess and ended up selling it to a customer!

Out of the blue, I was then approached by a local hotel who asked me if I could help them with their Twitter account as they weren't sure how to use it. They were my first client; I got that feeling again where I thought, 'Hang on, perhaps I have a business here'. People were willing to pay me to learn about Twitter and manage their accounts for them, as they didn't have time, and I realized I had a talent and more knowledge than I thought I had!

By talking to the followers they already had and building relationships with new customers, the hotel's clicks-to-sale went up 15 per cent. I saw that I could make a real impact and improve their sales, and this was how Tweeting Goddess was born.

The name is a play on Funky Goddess and seemed perfect for someone who was now managing people's Twitter accounts. Some people teased me about the Tweeting Goddess name. Online comments like 'Who does she think she is?' or 'She could do with losing a few pounds' were common, but I simply ignored them. The name has really worked for me. It's memorable – so memorable in fact that when some people meet me they don't call me Samantha, they call me Tweeting Goddess!

Since then I have built some awesome relationships on Twitter and spoken to (and met) people from all over the world. The conversations I start on Twitter with people I admire often progress to a Skype call or a coffee and a face-to-face chat.

Value for small business owners

Social media is extremely valuable for small business owners. The lovely thing about being a small business is that you can give a much more personal service. People buy from people, and that is one advantage that small business owners have; they can be more 'human'.

On Twitter, I find the best time to tweet is between 9 and 11 pm, when the kids are in bed and I have a little me-time. Most small and medium business (SMB) owners are the same: time poor, cash poor and juggling a family life with the uncertainties of running a business. For this reason many are online at this time too. So, if you are a business-to-business (B2B) service or product, that's when you should be online. Most big companies work 9 am to 5 pm, so small business owners can get ahead of the bigger competitors this way.

Small business owners don't have the big marketing budgets that others have, which means using social media is essential. It can provide the engagement that customers expect. It's vital to make sure you are on the right platform too, so make sure your desired audience are where you are.

Being on social media gives you a chance to do very valuable social listening. You can hear and see what is going on and where your competitors are and reach out to customers or potential customers who might need your service or product. This doesn't mean going straight for the sale immediately – instead, you can have a conversation and build relationships with them.

As a CEO or owner, it means so much to a customer that you are actually bothered to reply to them, adding that human element to the business. Showing what's going on behind the scenes is also always a good idea – people want to see that staff are being treated well and are happy.

Time is a major issue for business leaders, but it's important to set aside about fifteen minutes a day to respond to queries. Just go straight to your notifications to see who is interacting with you.

Twitter lists are a very useful way of keeping an eye on certain people you want to watch and also those whose content you enjoy. And if you have content or updates you would like to share, you can schedule these to go out a certain times – but always be ready to thank anyone who retweets or shares your content.

Top five tips for small business owners/entrepreneurs

1 Find out where your customers are, be it Twitter, Instagram, Facebook, Snapchat or LinkedIn. Twitter in particular is a great business-to-business platform, so start using it and see how many other CEOs are using it too.

2 Be yourself. Be human. People buy from people.

3 Keep your branding the same on all platforms so it's easy to find you.

4 Put out great tips and show your expertise. Show you are the 'go to person' for your industry.

5 Engage, engage, engage. Social media is meant to be social; it's not about putting out adverts. It's about educating, entertaining and building relationships that you can take further, be it a direct message, Skype call or coffee.

PART FOUR

THE FUTURE

25

Disrupt yourself

Matt Ballantine

In the summer of 2016 I found myself in the sleek marble, steel and glass offices of a City of London law firm. It was a stiflingly hot July evening, and the drinks were flowing as partners in the business celebrated the end of their annual gathering.

I was helping the organization to get a better handle on how digital would impact on how it operated and serviced its clients. Somehow I had managed to convince them to buy a virtual reality system and on that evening I was offering their senior lawyers the opportunity to immerse themselves at the bottom of a virtual ocean to swim with digital blue whales.

The response from people fell into one of three categories.

Some looked at what we were doing and haughtily scoffed that it was utterly irrelevant to the world of law.

Others looked at what was going on and asked me 'So what has this got to do with the world of law?' 'You tell me', I'd say to them. 'You're the lawyer!'

The final group looked at the system and asked if they could have a go. They explored it. They had fun, and then they started asking questions like 'I wonder how we could use this with clients to explain issues of health and safety law?' or 'I wonder if our real estate clients are using these types of technology yet?'

The firm's chief executive was firmly in the first category.

Back in the early 1990s, as an undergraduate in the School of Social Sciences at Loughborough University in the UK, I vividly remember the prognosis of our Information Systems lecturer about the future of what was a clutch of emerging new ways of navigating data on the internet. He saw much promise in WAIS and Gopher. He thought the new world wide web was a gimmick and couldn't see much of a future for it, especially given the expensive workstations on which it was required to run.

When a new technology emerges to the world, it's common for us to dismiss it, to fail to see how it might be of use or benefit. We see such new things as toys, and mostly in the world of work, we will dismiss them as such. This trait can be seen as much in experts in a field, as by the chief executives of law firms. Work is a serious thing, and toys are frivolous.

In hindsight, it is quite apparent that the world wide web was going to change the way we live in a way as profound as the telephone or the internal combustion engine. In hindsight, as I write this, it appears evident that 'virtual reality' is yet again a failure. By the time this book hits the shelves what will have happened? Well, only time will tell.

However, if there's one thing of which you can be assured, there's only one way in which you can practically make use of a toy. You play with it.

I am blessed to have two sons – lively, energetic, funny, curious and playful boys born thirteen months apart. They're best of friends for all of the time that they are not, and that can change like the wind. One of the things, though, that will almost always bring them together is Lego.

They can spend hour upon hour lost in their imaginations playing with Lego, and, over the past few years, I've observed that they have four main ways in which they interact with the toy.

The first, Battle Combat Mode, is where, in short, they throw it at each other. They are boys, they are thirteen short months apart in age and their moods change like the wind. They do it because the other is doing it. They have little idea why.

The second, IKEA Mode, is reminiscent of the way in which in adult life we construct flat-pack furniture from the Swedish home furnishing behemoth. The kids will select a model that they wish to build and then methodically follow the instructions until they have completed the three-dimensional jigsaw puzzle.

The third, Pokémon Mode, fuses Lego with another favourite from their world, the characters from the Japanese collector game. At present, there's no licensing deal between the two brands, so when the boys want to create a character, they need to work it out for themselves. They figure it out, piece by piece, and Pikachu or his friends duly emerge.

Finally – and as a child of the 1970s, where I still believe the spiritual heart of Lego lies – there is Tinkering Mode. The kids will go off into flights of imaginative fancy, creating characters and worlds on a whim.

As I have observed all of this play, my mind has drawn parallels with the worlds of activity and adoption of technology I see in the organizations with whom I have the privilege to work.

There's an awful lot of Battle Combat Mode. 'We need a Social Blockchain Big Data AI Machine Learning Bot!' comes the cry.

Why? Because our competitors are doing the same, and we have a fear of missing out. Or we have a fear of being seen as not innovative enough. Or we are just not confident enough to call out that the digital emperor is as naked as the day he was born.

There's a particular type of technology investment that I have taken to refer to as 'PR Tech' which is perfectly valid but serves no business purpose other than to build innovative credibility around a brand. In part, this is why so many businesses had their social presences run by interns for so long and, in the business-to-business (B2B) sector, many probably still do.

IKEA Mode is the way in which industrialized organizations grew and why so many of the things that surround you at this very moment exist. Develop repeatable, finessed best practices and processes and execute them with efficiency and effectiveness at scale.

This way of working is terrific. However, it breaks down if you don't know what you want or aren't sure if your way to solve a problem is the right way, or if a situation is new or novel or utterly ambiguous.

Pokemon Mode is often what organizations are trying to achieve when they talk about agility. You have a direction, but you have no way of knowing how to get there. So you take small steps and accept change and failure, limiting exposure to failure through assessing and learning and not being afraid to pull the plug entirely.

Agility is hard in any organization. It's hard because we have trained generation after generation to work in the ways described by the likes of FW Taylor and Henry Ford. We want certainty in outcomes, and agile approaches don't necessarily provide that. We talk about disruption and yet want anything but disruption. We talk about volatility, uncertainty, complexity and ambiguity but struggle desperately to account for any of them.

Which in turn brings us to Tinkering Mode. Without a doubt, the most depressing thing I have heard in the last few years was from the Head of Learning and Development at a client who told me, bluntly, that 'we don't have time for the luxury of play'.

However, if you don't make time to tinker, to play with the toys of emerging technology, then how will you or your organization ever be able to spot how to apply new things until after your competitors have already done so?

Don't get me wrong. Organizations can't operate if everyone is spending all of their time playing around with gadgets. You need to create a portfolio of activities that cover all bases. Moreover, that journey starts, for a leader, with the personal as well as the organizational. The tone that you set will be role-modelled throughout your business. If you are tinkering, you are giving implicit permission for others to do so. If you resolutely do not, you are closing the door for the whole organization.

There is no technology more pervasive or persuasive for setting the agenda for exploration and curiosity and change and innovation in business than social media, because everyone can see what you're doing.

And that, particularly for leaders who have been schooled to believe that their role is to be unambiguous and all-knowing, is fantastically disruptive. To not hide behind the ranks of corporate communicators, elegantly crafting messages to paint an illusion of the executive.

To survive in this chaotic, disruptive world of ours, you need to learn to disrupt yourself. Tinker with new things. Find out how they might fit into your world, and how they might evolve within your organization to provide benefit and competitive advantage.

This book provides a wealth of ideas about how you might do that. Here are some of the ideas I share with my clients about how to take steps towards tinkering with social as a senior executive.

Understand your work/not work continuum and concepts of formality

The boundaries between our work and our time outside of work are becoming increasingly blurred, especially as technology permeates deeper and deeper into our day-to-day lives. I'm not sure if there are clear distinctions any longer between a 'work/life balance'. But that doesn't mean that we can't make some mental separation in our minds which can help to provide context with different social channels.

There are no absolutes but personally I'd struggle to see how LinkedIn could be viewed as a place of leisure. Similarly, for me, Facebook is a place I tend to keep free of work conversations (although I know many for whom that is very much *not* the case).

I have WhatsApp channels for work and for friends and family. The streams rarely cross.

My blog is *mostly* about work but tends towards 'Working Out Loud' and is a description of the things that I am doing as I am doing them. It's raw and unpolished, deliberately so; my column for Forbes (essentially another blog) is much more carefully curated. Formal and informal and work and not work shouldn't be totally correlated.

Try to place where a social channel might sit in the work/not work spectrum and how formal a channel it is (and where that might or might not work for you). But then accept that as you start to explore any channel you will find out how it really works for you. That's the nature of tinkering.

Don't create a new, and poor, customer-service channel

A common fear when senior executives enter into the world of social is that the channel will become a new route by which disgruntled customers will vent their frustrations. There are two important things to take note of here.

The first is to establish routes by which any customer service issues can be triaged and dealt with quickly, effectively and – appropriately – publicly. That last point is important – if customers are taking to public channels to complain, resolution that happens in the background does nothing to bolster your corporate reputation.

But far more fundamentally, if you are fearful that by going online you will be opening yourself up to a flood of customer complaints, then *that* is the issue which you should be really concerning yourself – that is, what is so bad about your current service channels that customers are looking for ways to avoid them?

Don't just broadcast, engage

One of the best metaphors that I've heard to describe a social platform is my sometime colleague and CTO of transportation business Addison Lee Ian Cohen's description of Twitter as being like a pub. It's public. It's a place, primarily, of conversation. Some people know each other. Some are strangers. You'll probably find the odd drunken bore who just shouts at the furniture.

Don't be that drunken bore. Social channels are not, despite the best efforts of the traditional marketing industry, yet another media channel on which you push your messages. The power of social comes from engagement, not broadcasting. From being curious, humble and empathetic. From being, to coin a phrase, social.

The clue really is in the name.

Make it a habit

There is much spoken about how we are becoming addicted to technologies. We send people off on Digital Detoxes and install wellness applications onto their smartphones to regulate their addictions.

But at the other end of the spectrum, there is a broad cohort of senior leaders who seem to have unwittingly formed a digital temperance movement, abstaining entirely from the social world. We shouldn't forget that it's perfectly possible to form benign habits, and the effective use of social channels depends on it.

Build it into your day or week. Make time for it; otherwise it will never happen.

The single most useful habit that I have built into my own working pattern is that of the weeknote. Every Friday I spend a few minutes to write a short blog post that in no more than a few bullet points sums up the key things I've learned in the preceding seven days. It was an idea that I picked up from an article in *WIRED* magazine back in May 2010 and something that I have done habitually ever since. Ten minutes of my time, once a week, and it keeps those I know in touch with the things that I'm up to.

So there we have it. And so to work – it's time to get tinkering.

Work out loud. Start a blog. Tweet. Create a podcast.

Start conversations with customers, clients and suppliers.

Share what you are doing. Share how you are doing it.

Disrupt yourself. Become a social CEO.

Because if you can't do it with social networks, you won't stand a chance when it comes to the rest of the technologies that are going to turn your sector upside down.

26

The role of technology

Theo Priestley

Jack Ma, the former chairman and CEO of Alibaba, famously said in 2017 that he expected to see an artificial intelligence (AI) on the cover of *Time* magazine as 'CEO of the Year' by the year 2030.

In itself, the notion of a robotic AI leading a company within the next decade is both exciting and unsettling, driving home as it does just how fast technology is advancing. The likelihood that this will happen is, however, unlikely in my opinion – but there *are* examples where emerging technology has started to reshape the C-Suite agenda.

Bridgewater Associates, who manages the world's largest hedge fund, has already begun work to automate most of its senior management through algorithms. The founder, billionaire Ray Dalio, wanted to ensure that the firm continued to operate according to his guiding principles and vision even when he's no longer around.

Deep Knowledge Ventures (DKV), a Hong-Kong-based venture capital firm, appointed an AI to its Board of Directors in 2014. By

2017, 'Vital' (Validating Investment Tool for Advancing Life) was credited with bringing DKV back from the brink and work has already begun on Vital 2.0.

But why is this relevant or even important here?

This book is about how business leaders and the C-Suite must embrace more open and collaborative ways of engaging and interacting with the outside world, with clients, customers and supporters – as well as employees. With many higher level functions and complex decision-making starting to fall to the algorithm, this gives CEOs and their peers a unique opportunity to do exactly this – by affording them the time to explore how to lead and engage openly, from the front.

This isn't so much about what new platforms will be around in the next five years (it's extremely likely that the social media landscape that we know of today will change very little for business leaders) but about how new technology in the organization and boardroom will help advise the CEO *where* they should be spending their time online, and *how.*

There are many virtual assistants powered by machine learning algorithms which can learn your habits, check schedules and answer emails today. X.ai is a notable example that manages your diary and automatically answers requests to find the perfect slot for all parties concerned.

But what if the CEO used those same algorithms to understand how to become more communicative and social? Couldn't an algorithm learn the habits of the CEO and C-Suite, then adapt to teach business leaders how to react on social media to specific comments, feedback or in general become more open?

The short answer here is 'yes'.

A CEO could very easily train an algorithm without explicitly knowing they were doing so, through their emails, with the machine learning systems learning how the leader responds to scenarios or uses language in everyday contexts. In doing so, the systems could then suggest appropriate ways for the CEO to engage externally via social channels and suggest what to say.

This is not the same as social media automation which, put simply, is scheduling content in advance to make you appear active and engaging. What I'm suggesting is something that helps the CEO or senior leader to engage in a style and tone that the machine has learnt from them – a bit like a set of training wheels on a bicycle. In this way it could be used to aid and ease business leaders into the role of being more social without them being thrown into the deep end or have a public relations (PR) department prescribe what must be said.

What's more, an algorithm won't be as arbitrary as a PR-driven exercise or automation software because it won't suggest 'scattergun' techniques (posting on every channel). More often than not it is immediately transparent when a CEO has actually written a post themselves or not, simply by monitoring the frequency, where they've posted and whether they've even bothered to engage with replies. An algorithm could very well help the CEO with all of this.

Of course, it's easy to wax lyrical about AI and completely ignore other emerging trends.

Good old messaging

Email, for example, remains an important communication tool that every CEO and business leader can't ignore, but the rise of instant messaging and collaboration tools is also important as a means of becoming more social and responsive. Whether it's WhatsApp, Skype IM, Slack, Teams – or even Twitter and LinkedIn direct messages – the ability to communicate and collaborate one to one or one to many using these tools is an absolute must for any CEO wishing to move with the times.

While it may seem like unnecessary additional layers of distraction, only the CEO knows just how much time they can devote to it – but for internal visibility beyond simply firing off monthly emails across the company, it's golden.

Virtual interaction

Despite misgivings of my own, virtual environments may well one day begin to fulfil their promise of visual collaboration and interaction at levels not seen before. Whether through virtual reality, augmented reality or, more realistically, holographic technology (which will surpass both as a workplace and collaboration/communication tool), any CEO looking to understand the future landscape of engagement must start here.

The ability to communicate and respond remotely as if you were in the room is just too good an opportunity to ignore. Many platforms already exist which allow environments to be created where you can stand before large numbers of people and speak or interact. While they may seem clunky today, in the next five years the transition from communicating in the real world to a virtual environment could very well become seamless.

Coupled with machine learning and holographic representation, could we see virtual CEOs taking the reins going forward? Who knows, but if we already have virtual newsreaders then anything is possible!

Recorded for posterity?

One could argue that as we try to become a more transparent and balanced society, transparency and accountability need to be recorded. Could CEOs see themselves investing in a blockchain solution where every social interaction is recorded and never deleted from public record? Perhaps!

Mistakes are always made (Elon Musk's Twitter interactions and proclamations provide a valuable case study), but an immutable record would make any CEO and business leader think twice before interacting socially. This may be off-putting for a lot of people. However, being able to carry that record to a new business as proof of open and social leadership could be an invaluable asset in years to come when being 'social' may become a job requirement for CEOs and other senior leaders.

In all, I don't expect the social media landscape to alter drastically in the next five years or so. Many other new channels have risen and fallen in the last five years and, for a social CEO, it's not a question of wanting to jump onto every new platform over the next decade, but to evaluate and use the ones that make the most sense for them – and their audiences.

The future for a social-minded CEO is looking more rewarding than it has been thus far, because it will become *more* accessible through emerging technology, not harder as a result of it. Above all else, when evaluating these emerging trends as a means to becoming more engaging and interactive with employees, customers and supporters, any CEO must ask one overriding question before taking a leap into the unknown: 'Does this still make me human?'

27

The future of leadership

Michelle Carvill

In 1996 I ventured to business school to undertake a Master's in Business. Every book on the reading list and every lecture I attended included the concept of 'the paradigm shift' – 'an important change that happens when the usual way of thinking about or doing something is replaced by a new and different way'.[1]

Over the last twenty years this sometimes-overplayed corporate management term has truly played out, and there's now no denying that business has changed more quickly and dramatically than at any other time since the Industrial Revolution. The internet has totally revolutionized the way we connect and communicate.

We've seen technological advancements that have changed the way we work, learn, connect and communicate in ways that, not so long ago, would have seemed more like science fiction.

Self-driving cars, wearable tech, smart devices, the Internet of Things (IoT), crypto, blockchain, augmented reality (AR), artificial intelligence (AI) and the quest for 'conscious' robots (as I witnessed recently when meeting the enchanting (and just a tad creepy) Sophia the Robot). Suffice to say, we're only just scratching the surface when it comes to how humans and machines collaborate.

As discussed throughout this book, social technologies have played a big part in changing the way in how we connect and communicate.

While many still refer to social media as 'new', if we think about the pace of change – and just how long the majority of social networks have actually been active (which ranges between twelve and fifteen years) – it's clear to see that (1) they are not so 'new' after all and (2) they have clearly been key enablers in driving collaborative connection and conversation.

At the time of writing, more than three billion people around the world choose social networks as their preferred mode to connect and converse daily. And thanks to mobile technology and the ease of accessing these networks – and the simplicity and fun aspect of engaging via social networks – the number of hours a day people actually spend connecting and conversing continues to increase. Currently sitting at around two to two and a half hours a day – and closer to three and a half hours a day in some demographics – social media is a significant part of our daily 'online' attention.

From an 'expectation' perspective, it's simple to tune in and communicate with people, regardless of who they are – be they a world leader, a CEO, a member of royalty or a celebrity.

Any barriers to entry are nowadays well and truly broken down. The ordinary person is a broadcaster, interviewer and potential influencer, with an ever-increasing expectation to be heard. Our conscious and socially mobilized consumers, influencers, employees, stakeholders and potential consumers all have an expectation to be able to converse with just about anyone.

Greater expectations

Similar to the continuous learning afforded by AI, we clever humans have absorbed and embraced these new technologies and have adapted into what I like to refer to as 'Superpowered People'.

We've moved beyond being merely savvy and 'hyper-connected' consumers. Our 'consciousness' is now playing a part in our expectation of the roles that organizations, brands and leaders play. We now expect them – especially the leaders – to solve much bigger problems than speedier response times to questions or gripes via Twitter.

In 2017, Edelman's study 'Beyond No Brand's Land', with 14,000 respondents across fourteen countries, identified that 57 per cent of consumers are buying or boycotting brands based on the brand's position on a social or political issue – 30 per cent more than three years earlier.

Brandfog's 'Brands and Stands: Social Purpose is the New Black' report found that, of the 64 per cent of those who believe that it's extremely important for a company to take a stand on social issues, they were also very likely to purchase a product based on that commitment.

For our ever-increasing superpowered people, silence is not an option. The report adds that 67 per cent bought a brand for the first time because of its position on a controversial or social issue, and 65 per cent stated that they would not buy a brand if it stayed silent on an issue it had an obligation to address.

In the UK, thanks to a noisy backlash on social media surrounding a banned Christmas Advert by the food discount retail chain Iceland,[2] in which the company struck a deal with Greenpeace to broadcast an animated short film about the effect of palm oil production on orangutans (which then escalated across the majority of UK media outlets, both on and offline), I – newly educated and curious about their much publicized and celebrated environmental stance – visited one of their stores for the first time and made a number of purchases, having walked past it for the previous fifteen years. My behaviour nestled nicely into the above '67 per cent bought a brand for the first time' statistic.

All change

What does all this change mean for leaders and the future of leadership?

In many ways everything has changed, and yet nothing has changed. Our inherent desire to connect, communicate and progress remains the same. It's just the landscape, tools and expectations that have evolved.

'Superpowered people', regardless of demographics (although more prevalent in those generations waiting to rise through the ranks), are more comfortable challenging and questioning authority. They also dismiss hierarchy and demand straight-talking honesty from those we trust to run our organizations, countries and lives.

By superpowered people I mean your customers, your employees, your stakeholders, your supporters, your investors, your competitors, your competitors' employees and customers, your potential customers, your potential employees, your family, your peers and your friends. Effectively, people. Period.

#FollowTheLeader

To lead, you need people to follow you. And in the age of the connected superpowered human, there is a growing desire for leaders to drop the 'locked away, hidden from view' command and control stance and become more collaborative, open, accessible and transparent. They need to lead from the front, both internally and externally.

We have already witnessed an increasing number of CEOs and leaders being 'called out' by the public on social media. In a world fogged by 'fake news', people (and, again, that means both employees and external stakeholders) want to hear news, updates and what's really going on directly from the 'horse's mouth'.

For leaders, this means metaphorically stepping out of the boardroom and, from an internal perspective, stepping into the open plan office, walking the floor, being accessible, interested, caring and transparent; and for an external audience, it means stepping out into the spotlight and doing exactly the same. Overall, it means being fully 'tuned in' and accountable – reconnecting the disconnect and building trust.

Talking of trust

In 2017, The Edelman Trust Barometer reported that trust in CEOs was at an all-time low of just 37 per cent. A year later, their 'The Battle for Truth' 2018 Trust Barometer showed a small rise in trust in CEOs (rising to 43 per cent) attributed to the impact of more leaders and experts speaking out against 'fake news'.

What I think is more interesting, however, is the statistic that 70 per cent believed the number one role of the CEO is to build trust in their organization.

To build trust, it's no longer good enough to leave all corporate communications and customer service communications in the polished (and often over-scripted) hands of the customer-service, marketing, public relations and communications teams.

Communication is personal. There's an expectation from audiences, both internal (employees, colleagues) and external, to have more direct and open conversations with the people who lead them or who lead the organizations they care about or buy from. Indeed, Brandfog's 2016 Brand Reputation and Leadership Trust report identified that

- 78 per cent of people would prefer to work for an organization whose leadership is active on social media and

- 81 per cent believed that CEOs who engage in social media are better equipped than their peers to lead an organization in this digital age.

What's stopping you?

So, given our changing landscape and all the evidence contained within this book, the question is this: What's stopping more leaders from getting involved?

From my experience, key challenges usually focus around these four areas:

- Overwhelm – not clear on how to use the technologies, what to say or how to say it

- Time – don't have the time to fit social media into their working day

- Return on investment (ROI) – unclear of justifying the actual return on investment

And last, but most certainly not least – and encompassing all of the above reasons:

- Fear – fear of getting it wrong, fear of making a fool of themselves, fear of losing face, fear of saying the wrong thing, fear of no one engaging, fear of making mistakes.

Overwhelm, ROI and time (and indeed some aspects of fear) can all be accounted for with good training, processes, guidelines and support. After all, the channels themselves have been designed to be as user friendly as possible – and are all easily accessible via apps on your smartphone.

Fear is the biggest challenge for many – and I've coached a handful of leaders totally anonymously for this very reason. But, of course, these fears are not purely the domain of social media. The bigger challenge for leaders is that such fears are indeed a very real component of the traditional command and control leadership environment. In this environment, there isn't the culture (or safety net) to get creative and vulnerable and collaborate and ask others for help.

Stepping up, stepping out and sharing your voice in an authentic way takes a mindset shift and sometimes a cultural shift. And that often takes a bit longer. But in a world where communication and expectation continue to change at a blistering speed, those that fold their arms and say 'not for me' are going to continue to fall even further behind those already embracing change.

There's nothing quite like 'doing' to overcome fear. And social media offers you the perfect opportunity to listen and learn – to tune in to what your audience, your peers and those you admire are saying and doing in the social media space.

I'm a big advocate of learning from others as there's nothing quite like real-world experience. This is why, when researching my book *Get Social*, like Damian I also interviewed a number of leaders who really do 'get' social and see their time and activity on these channels as fundamental to their own development and the development of the organizations they work for or lead.

Like many have already cited in earlier chapters, these are leaders that have stepped outside their comfort zones. They have shared how they manage their time, their content, their message, their engagement and their ups and downs – all in a way that fits into their life and brings value and, fundamentally, a return to their business.

So here are some useful lessons I learned from them – lessons that are likely to be useful for you too:

1   Listen. Without exception, all leaders I interviewed cited 'listening' as a key benefit of their social media activity. Getting close to the front line, staying tuned in. Brian J Dunn, former CEO of Best Buy and a pioneering social CEO, told me: 'Listening in helps me to see round corners.' Being 'tuned in' and 'contextual' is most definitely a leadership trait to nurture.

2   Master one channel at a time. You don't have to do it all. Figure out what makes sense for you, be objectively driven, choose the right tools for the job and do one thing really well. And then, if relevant, move on to other things.

3   Weave it into your life. Being 'social' is something you *are* rather than something you *do*. Build your activity into your life. Review your feeds over breakfast, catch up on the latest news and updates when travelling or commuting – or block twenty minutes out of your diary in the morning and afternoon to check what's happening. Make tuning in and conversing a part of what you do. Just like sending an email, checking your social channels should become part of your day-to-day activity. As John Legere, CEO of T-Mobile USA, told me, 'Any leader that doesn't make time for social media is missing a huge opportunity.'

4   Get support. You're not on your own, and nor do you need to be. The landscape has changed and learning how these tools can help you become a better leader is part of leadership development. Get 'authentic' – you can't know it all. This is my world and I don't know it all. There's no shame in that. Ask your leadership and development teams for help, find the right courses, training, coaching, support. Collaborate with others. Kevin Burrowes, Head of Clients and Markets at PwC, told me that he plans time with his PA weekly to review his social media activity, getting help with content, managing his plan and finding ideas and topical news to share.

5   Be authentic. It has to be you. Your social activity has to be your voice. Again, without exception, every leader I interviewed told me just how important it is that the bulk of any engagement is done by them. Your views, your voice. While you can – and indeed should – get all the support

you need, your voice really isn't something you should be outsourcing.

My view, and indeed the views of the leaders I interviewed and continue to interview and talk with, is that being active on social media makes for a better leader. For me, social media literacy and the future of leadership are inextricably linked.

When determining social media literacy, from my perspective, it is these social behaviours that are most important. They are simply facilitated by technology:

- Collaboration
- Consciousness/tuning in
- Customer, stakeholder and employee engagement
- Co-creation
- Communication
- Transparency
- Accessibility
- Authenticity

These are traits that could also be defined as key skills for the modern leader.

While I've read a lot about the changing face of leadership, greater minds than mine talk about the skills required for this new age of leadership. The brilliant book *Why Should Anyone Be Led By You* by Rob Goffee and Gareth Jones, and indeed *4D Leadership* and *Coherence* by Dr Alan Watkins, are some of many that very much align with my own thinking and beliefs around what it now takes to be a great leader.

Around ten years ago, I recall reading a piece of research from Cisco predicting that the leaders of the future would be those that were the most 'socially enabled'. There are significant parallels between what it takes to succeed on social media and what it takes to be an effective leader today and in the future.

I therefore stand by my hypothesis that getting social really does aid and teach you to become a better leader.

Yet, to echo the sentiment of Brian Solis in the foreword to this book, social technologies are purely systems. It's how you fuel them that really matters. And that comes from you.

I'll end with a warning that, whether on social media or in leadership, you can't fake sincerity.

Conclusion

Damian Corbet

Transparent. Open. Honest. Engaged. Community-minded.

These are some of the leadership qualities that come shining through the chapters of this book. They are qualities that today's social CEOs hold close to their hearts. They live and work in the open; they engage with their communities – internally and externally; they share their ideas and values; they admit their mistakes.

This is revolutionary stuff. It's hard to imagine CEOs twenty or thirty years ago behaving like this. They'd probably have been laughed out of the boardroom.

The fact is, however, that CEOs who think like this are still in the minority. They are the risk-takers, the early adopters, the vanguard of a new type of leadership. They may be in the minority now, but believe me, they won't be in five years. In the Social Age, these qualities will soon be a requirement.

The advent of social media has totally revolutionized the way organizations operate – or will have to operate in the near future. And this extends to the leaders of these organizations. Gone are the days of obscure official pronouncements and controlled messages. With so many people now having access to the internet, information flows freely across the world. When something interesting or important or bad happens somewhere in the world, it's only a matter of seconds before someone shares it on Twitter, Instagram or Facebook.

This was demonstrated in such an awful way with the live Facebook streaming of the mosque shootings in Christchurch, New Zealand, in March 2019. That is an extreme example – and the social media giants are, belatedly, putting in place new controls to stop this kind of content being viewed and shared – but it is a stark reminder of the power of social media to bypass all the official news channels.

The same can happen with bad news about an organization. Your organization.

A petroleum company dealing with a major oil spill? A charity facing allegations of illegal fundraising practices? A municipal authority accused of squandering public funds on inefficient public projects? A food company mired in a contamination scandal? The list of potential crises is endless – as are the opportunities for the news to be shared far and wide on social media. How will you, as the CEO or senior leader, cope? Will you try to hide, or will you put your head above the parapet and face things head on?

Of course crises have always been a part of life for organizations and their leaders. It's nothing new. What is new is the way the news can spread around the world in seconds. In the past, when organizations had more control over the message, they dealt with crises in more 'traditional' ways: press conferences, a series of corporate press releases, perhaps even a ban on employees speaking to the press. If things got really bad the CEO may have been hauled before the cameras to explain things – with varying degrees of success.

Who remembers the CEO of BP, Tony Hayward, after the Deepwater Horizon disaster in 2010, appearing evasive and saying he 'wanted his life back' – after eleven people died in the initial explosion and two more died during the clean up? Not good PR. Not good leadership. Old-fashioned leadership that didn't understand – although social media wasn't as prevalent then as it is now – that the world was changing and the 'message' had to be genuine.

Compare that with the reaction of Tony Fernandez, CEO of Air Asia, after the crash of Flight QZ 8501 in 2014, with the loss of all lives on board. He was straight on Twitter, sending his condolences and providing updates on the subsequent investigation. His tweets were genuine and heartfelt – typos and all. This was not corporate PR followed by a reluctant appearance before the cameras by the CEO. This was modern leadership for the Social Age.

Of course CEOs and other senior leaders still need to understand and master all the core leadership skills required for running an organization. That's a given. But what leaders these days need to understand is that the old ways of doing things – as taught in leadership schools – are no longer enough. Leaders need to do more. They need to be prepared for the Social Age. Not just be prepared – they need to *embrace* it.

'Directors who don't understand social media are placing their company at risk of not capitalizing on the business opportunities, as well as exposing it to unnecessary risk.' Those are the words of Australian customer experience expert Walter Adamson in an article he wrote back in 2014.[1] He got it then. How many leaders still don't get it today?

Writer and researcher Julian Stodd sums things up well in his book *The Social Leadership Handbook* where he says: 'Social leadership isn't an optional extra: it's a method and mindset for engaging in communities and deploying the power of your organization that liberates innovation and creativity. Organizations that lack this power will feel increasingly less relevant in the Social Age.'[2]

The key word is 'mindset'.

Social leadership is all about mindset. It's not simply about having LinkedIn, Twitter or Instagram accounts. These are important, but they're just tools – and it's not the tools that make you a social leader, it's how you use them. What matters is understanding the potential of these tools to change the world. Approach things with the right mindset – one that sees openness, interaction and collaboration as advantages, not scary things to be avoided – and suddenly your social media tools take on magical powers.

So, it's time to leave the corner office, step into the digital lobby and engage with the people that affect your organization. Be transparent, open, honest, engaged and community-minded. The effect is exhilarating.

Good luck on your social leadership journey!

NOTES

Introduction

1 Jan Owen—A CEO Using Social Media To Help Young People (https://medium.com/the-social-c-suite/jan-owen-a-ceo-using-social-media-to-help-young-people-5e4077ff913d).

Chapter 2

1 Six social-media skills every leader needs, McKinsey Quarterly, Roland Deiser and Sylvain Newton, February 2013.

2 https://www.slideshare.net/AndreaTEdwards/success-story-unleash-your-employees-disrupt-from-within-grow-your-business-103390123

3 https://www.edelman.com/trust-barometer

Chapter 4

1 Why I Sometimes Ask for Help from a 5-Year-Old (https://www.linkedin.com/pulse/mind-skills-gap-why-i-sometimes-ask-help-from-bob-nardelli/).

2 In This Candid Conversation, Legendary CEO John Chambers Reveals the Critical Skill Leaders Need Now (https://www.forbes.com/sites/carminegallo/2018/12/04/in-this-candid-conversation-legendary-ceo-john-chambers-reveals-the-critical-skill-leaders-need-now/#543e28b56cb0).

Chapter 5

1 UK Cabinet Office. MINDSPACE, Influencing behaviour through public policy. Available at: https://www.instituteforgovernment.org.uk/sites/default/files/publications/MINDSPACE.pdf. Date accessed: 07 March 2019.

2 Helen Prosser. Family Practice. Influences on GPs' decision to prescribe new drugs – the importance of who says what. Available at: https://academic.oup.com/fampra/article/20/1/61/498919. Date accessed: 07 March 2019.

3 McKinsey and Company. What beauty players can teach the consumer sector about digital disruption. Available at: https://www.mckinsey.com/industries/consumer-packaged-goods/our-insights/what-beauty-players-can-teach-the-consumer-sector-about-digital-disruption. Date accessed: 07 March 2019.

4 Ibid.

5 Hans Detlefsen. Airbnb's Market Share of U.S. Lodging Demand Increasing at a Decelerating Rate. Available at: https://www.hotel-online.com/press_releases/release/airbnbs-market-share-of-u.s.-lodging-demand-increasing-at-a-decelerating-ra. Date accessed: 07 March 2019.

6 Ofcom. Adults' Media Use and Attitudes Report 2018. Available at: https://www.ofcom.org.uk/__data/assets/pdf_file/0011/113222/Adults-Media-Use-and-Attitudes-Report-2018.pdf. Date accessed: 07 March 2019.

7 Ibid.

8 Ibid.

9 Raconteur. Over 50s market prefers 'enhancement' to anti-ageing. Available at: https://www.raconteur.net/retail/over-50s-market-prefers-enhancement-to-anti-ageing. Date accessed: 07 March 2019.

10 Ibid.

11 Digiday. The demographics of YouTube, in 5 charts. Available at: https://digiday.com/media/demographics-youtube-5-charts/. Date accessed: 07 March 2019.

12 Ibid.

13 McKinsey and Company. What beauty players can teach the consumer sector about digital disruption.

14 Evening Standard. Charlotte Tilbury make-up brand looks good after sales jump. Available at: https://www.standard.co.uk/business/charlotte-tilbury-makeup-brand-looks-good-after-sales-jump-a3951261.html. Date accessed: 07 March 2019.

15 Kelly Pinol, DRG. Taking the Pulse Europe 2016. EU5 Physicians Summary Deck.

16 Ibid.

17 Ibid.

Chapter 6

1 https://whatis.techtarget.com/definition/social-media

2 Andresen Horowitz 'Mobile is eating the world'.

3 Alliance Magazine, 18 August 2018

4 WWF June 2018.

Chapter 9

1 https://www.mpsontwitter.co.uk

2 https://www.socialceos.org/

Chapter 10

1 Beware the angry birds, *The Economist*, 11 October 2014. https://www.economist.com/business/2014/10/11/beware-the-angry-birds

Chapter 14

1 The Social CEOs Award (http://www.socialceos.org/) recognizes and celebrates charity leaders who are using social media and digital to propel their charity forward.

2 Marmite is a British food spread made from yeast extract, a by-product of beer brewing. It famously advertises itself as being either 'loved or hated'.

Chapter 19

1 Clearing is a way for British universities to fill any spaces they have left for the upcoming academic year. It takes place in the summer and gives applicants who do not hold an offer another chance of finding a university place.

2 Paul Daniels was an English magician and television presenter. He achieved international fame through his television series 'The Paul Daniels Magic Show', which ran on the BBC from 1979 to 1994. He died in 2016.

3 Toby Young is a British journalist and formerly Director of the New Schools Network, a free schools charity. He is currently the London associate editor at *Quillette*. He has come under criticism for comments made on Twitter, most of which were subsequently deleted.

4 The Oyster card is an electronic ticket used on public transport in Greater London in the UK.

Chapter 24

1 Derek Edward Trotter, more commonly known as Del Boy, is the fictional lead character in the popular BBC sitcom Only Fools and Horses.

2 *Dragons' Den* is a British television programme where entrepreneurs get an opportunity to present their business ideas to a panel of five wealthy investors, the 'Dragons', and pitch for financial investment while offering a stake of the company in return.

Chapter 27

1 https://www.merriam-webster.com/dictionary/paradigm per cent20shift

2 https://www.theguardian.com/media/2018/nov/09/iceland-christmas-tv-ad-banned-political-greenpeace-orangutan

Conclusion

1 https://www.linkedin.com/pulse/20140404084700-17730-c-suite-social-media-training-misses-the-point/

2 *The Social Leadership Handbook*, Julian Stodd, 22 July 2016.

INDEX